HCP Publishing

San Francisco, California

2013

Copyright Information

The Healthy Husband Cookbook:

How To Feed The Man You Love
Good Food and Good Health

Helen Cassidy Page

A How To Cook Healthy In A Hurry Cookbook

Free Gift

Before we get started, check out the How To Cook Healthy website below to get my gift to you of 5 free, delicious, sugar-free dessert recipes and receive e-mail updates, promotions and tidbits on eating and living well.

http://www.helencassidypage.com/how-to-cook-healthy-in-a-hurry-bonus/

Please Review

Give The Healthy Husband Cookook A Thumbs Up

Most cooks agree that a cookbook is worth the price if you find even one recipe that becomes a favorite. I hope you will find many recipes that will please you and make your kitchen life easier. If you do, please help me spread the word about The Healthy Husband Cookbook. Tell your friends and please give it a positive review on Amazon by going to this website:

http://www.amazon.com/The-Healthy-Husband-Cookbook-Recipes-Health-ebook/dp/B00BEBOW8K/

Happy Eating

Helen

Get all the books in the series:

How To Cook Healthy In A Hurry, Volume 1

eBook version:

http://www.amazon.com/How-Cook-Healthy-Hurry-Recipes-ebook/dp/B00AP980WG/

Paperback version:
www.createspace.com/4318842

My first book in this series offers 50 delicious recipes that require less than 30 minutes in the kitchen and are packed with flavor and nutrition. I even have a testimonial from a 7 year old that his favorite dinner is from this cookbook.

How To Cook Healthy In A Hurry, Volume 2

eBook version:

http://www.amazon.com/How-To-Cook-Healthy-Hurry-ebook/dp/B00C3OHEGE

Paperback version:
www.createspace.com/4517744

How To Cook Healthy In A Hurry, Volumes 1 and 2

eBook version:

http://www.amazon.com/HOW-COOK-HEALTHY-HURRY-MINUTES-VOLUMES-ebook/dp/B00DFN0LDA/

Paperback version:
www.createspace.com/4337541

For your convenience, all the recipes in How To Cook Healthy In A Hurry Volumes 1 and 2 are compiled into one book.

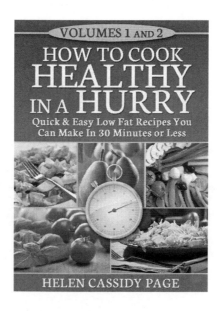

The Soup Diet Cookbook

eBook version:

shttp://www.amazon.com/Soup-Diet-Cookbook-Delicious-ebook/dp/B00BRRZQC2/

Paperback version:
www.createspace.com/4404701

What is the number one problem with losing weight? Hunger pangs. The Soup Diet Cookbook is based on scientific research that shows that certain types of soup eaten at certain times will help ward off hunger. You can lose weight without changing the food you love if you follow The South Diet Cookbook and enjoy the delicious soups and smoothies here.

Table of Contents

DEDICATION

Dedicated to Dr. Stephen Blumlein, Dr. Vincent Gaudiani, Dr. Glenn Egrie and Dr. Sachin Shah, and their colleagues and staff, in fact, all the wonderful people at California Pacific Medical Center who keep my heart, my health and my spirits in tip top shape. I can't begin to tell you all how much I appreciate you all.

Introduction: The $350,000 Dinner

When you think about it, it's really not that hard to put a quick, mouthwatering dinner together. Stick a baked potato in the oven, throw a thick steak on the grill and make sure you have your favorite ice cream in the freezer for dessert. When the steak is ready, melt a pat of butter or blue cheese on top, slather the potato with butter, sour cream and bacon bits and stick a strawberry on the ice cream just to add some color.

Then sit back and watch your husband devour his $350,000 meal.

Wait, you're asking. Where did the $350,000 come from?

Well, that's what his possible bypass surgery may cost in a few years, not counting lost time at work, the terror and discomfort after the operation and the changes to his lifestyle he could have been making now that would have helped avoid the surgery. Or, this could be you if you join him in this lifestyle. After all, heart attacks are the leading cause of death among women in the United States, with equally high rates in other countries. But let's just talk about men for now.

Not to be a wet blanket as I start out a book that is supposed to be about enjoying great food, but we have to do something about the typical Western diet. It is killing the men we love.

You probably know this already. It is fairly common knowledge that heart attacks kill 1 in 4 people every year. So count off your beloved friends, family, and particularly your spouse. You will probably lose one-fourth of them prematurely. Who should go first?

Enough Of The Bad Cop Routine, Here Comes The Good Cop

Why do we continue to eat the foods that are so bad for us? That's easy. Because they taste so good. Because it's hard to change our eating habits. Because nobody wants to give up eating food that we love, dishes that our mothers raised us on, meals that we equate with family, friends and good times. I don't know about you, but I certainly don't. But the alternative isn't so great either. I know first hand.

As I write this I am recovering from open-heart surgery. It was almost laughable when I got the news. Me, who has been writing about the urgency of a heart-healthy lifestyle for decades. Well, about seventeen years ago I was told that I had a heart murmur, that is, I had a defective aortic valve, the gizmo that helps regulate blood flow to and from the heart. There was no remedy for it, no change in my lifestyle or diet could repair it. Medication wouldn't help, and I didn't cause it by eating the wrong foods, or smoking or spending my life on the couch instead of exercising. It was just Mother Nature having a laugh at my expense. The valve would either stay the same and not cause any problems, or get worse over time. If it deteriorated, eventually I would have to have a valve job.

It was a wait and see proposition, so I promptly went out and completed my first (and only) marathon. I had no symptoms and my doctor put no restrictions on my activities. The years passed and while my cardiologist kept tabs on my heart, nothing much changed. For a long time. Then the news became worrisome. The opening in the valve was getting smaller, and my heart was having to work too hard to pump blood. I wasn't at crisis stage. Yet. But it was coming. But I felt fine. More years passed and even when the reports showed the valve was deteriorating even more, I had no symptoms, so I refused to think about surgery. Until several months ago when I needed a relatively minor surgical procedure for something else. I showed up for my pre-op exam a week before the scheduled surgery. To my great shock, I didn't pass go, and I didn't get a get out of jail free card. Instead, I got an appointment with a heart surgeon.

I was told that I might not survive the surgery unless I had my heart fixed first. Picture me panicked and in tears as I left that office to call my friend and co-author, a noted cardiologist at Stanford University. We'd written two heart healthy cookbooks together. He reviewed my test and said, yes, you have to have this surgery. Now!!!!!

So what does this have to do with you? And your husband? The subject is heart disease, not bad valves. Well, in my crash course on fixing broken hearts, I learned that by the time people with my condition need surgery, their arteries are often diseased as well. At this point they require not one but two surgeries. And we're not talking fixing a hangnail, here. These are big assaults on the body. The first one repairs the clogged arteries and then the second operation replaces the valve. Some surgeons perform them at the same time, but my surgeon, who is one of the best, does not recommend that. He does them one at a time. If my arteries were clogged with plaque, I would have a bypass, then when I recovered, I'd go back for an aortic valve replacement. So I waited for the test results to tell me if I was in for double dipping, one or two heart surgeries.

It Shouldn't Have Happened To Me

I started out my cooking and writing career as a French chef. I worshipped at the altar of Julia Child and had made huge investments in butter and cream over the years. Then my friend at Stanford asked me to write a low-cholesterol cookbook with him. I literally said, "Sure, but what's cholesterol?"

For the next year, I did research and found out. It didn't take long to convince me that I had to cool it with the butter and cream. On the other hand, I consoled myself with the discovery that there are so many ways to cook great food and so many fabulous things to eat that I didn't have to feel deprived. As far as the changes in my diet were concerned, if I were going to practice what I preached, I was just going to trade some really good things that might harm me for some other really good things that were better for me.

Over the years I have certainly enjoyed my share of rich food, though I've basically kept to the program. Yet, when I went in to have the test that would determine whether I needed one or two surgeries, I was very, VERY nervous. Heart disease runs in my family. Even with the healthiest lifestyle, there was still a risk that, even without symptoms, I could have artery disease.

However, I was an advocate for healthy eating. This shouldn't be happening to me. And, in fact, fortunately, it wasn't. My arteries were clear. And

20

thank goodness for that. Because now, not quite three months after my valve surgery, I am still recovering. And I can tell you that one invasive heart operation is enough. Yes, I'm eternally grateful that Dr. Gaudiani saved my life (He's the best. I recommend you see him if you need heart surgery-he's in the San Francisco Bay Area). But you don't want heart surgery if you don't have to have it.

Bypass surgery and aortic valve replacement procedures are slightly different, but the effect on the body and the recovery period is basically the same, which gives me great empathy for any cardiac surgery patient. And the good news for you and your husband, is that unlike me with a broken heart, you can take steps to avoid surgery and/or a heart attack. The risk of heart disease is dramatically lowered by simple changes in the typical sedentary lifestyle and western meat and processed foods-heavy diet. The one so many husbands like to eat.

But of course heart disease is not the only problem for the men we love and the food they love to eat. A diet crammed with animal fat, processed foods, too much sugar and white flour and not enough healthy nutrition leads to diabetes, obesity, which, among other things, puts excess pressure on the spine and knee joints. This way of eating can lead to high blood pressure and kidney disease. The good news: you, your husband, or anyone can help prevent all this can by committing to five healthy lifestyle changes.

The Five Principles Of A Healthy Husband Lifestyle

A healthy husband lifestyle (or a healthy human lifestyle for that matter) means a commitment to five principles (where have you heard this before):

* No smoking
* Daily exercise
* Maintaining a healthy weight
* Controlling stress (rather than have it control you)
* Eating a healthy diet

We can't control our genes or the random indifference of fate when it comes to our health. Some families have a predisposition for certain diseases. You can't undo your genes to lower that risk (though a healthy lifestyle might reduce it). Or, we find ourselves in the wrong place at the wrong time and we catch a nasty virus. That's life.

However, people (such as your beloved) who can make a commitment to these five principles listed above as much as possible (see the 80/20 rule below), can dramatically reduce their risk of developing what I call lifestyle diseases. Those are the heart attacks, strokes, diabetes, bad knees, and so forth caused by obesity, a high animal fat and inflammation-producing diet and a sedentary, stressful and smoke-filled lifestyle. Those are unhealthy habits and aspects of our lives that we choose. In fact, they are the only aspects of our lives that we can fully control.

Of these five principles, it is the last one, the healthy diet, that the family cook can influence. And that is the one this book will address.

Help Your Favorite Husband Three Ways

The recipes in The Healthy Husband Cookbook will help your husband in three ways:

By reducing animal fats, which are shown to contain unhealthy amounts of heart attack causing-saturated fat;

By reducing the inflammation-producing processed foods that always seem to fall off the supermarket shelves into our grocery carts and contribute to many diseases;

And by using an abundance of so-called superfoods, those items that really punch up the nutrition quotient of our meals and provide disease-fighting vitamins and minerals our bodies need.

Whether You Have A Husband, Are A Husband Or Know A Husband, This Book Is For You!

While I don't have scientific evidence to back this up, it has been my observation that men have a different relationship to food than women do. Yes, women can enjoy steaks and ice cream and pizza, all things men love. But the reverse isn't always true. Men can shy away from "girly food." You know, salads, fish, fruit and veggies, in favor of a man-sized burger and fries.

But it is also true that while many men cook for themselves, their wives and their families, women still prepare most of the meals we eat. Consequently, women have a lot of influence on

23

the diets of the men they love. And that's why I'm talking to women. But you men out there? Feel free to listen in. 'Cause I'm talkin' to you, too. Whether you have a husband, are a husband or know a husband, this book is for you!

It Doesn't Matter If You Have A Young Husband Or A Not So Young Husband

Many people think they only need to start watching their diets when they get older, if at all. However, research has shown that the plaque that leads to artery disease shows up in children as young as six years old. Diabetes and high blood pressure can also make an early appearance. The message is loud and clear. You are never too young to start taking care of your heart or any other part of your body. Or that of the men you care about, husbands and sons. Fathers, brothers and friends.

And the care and feeding of a healthy husband isn't just about his heart. Obesity, smoking, lack of exercise and stress all put your husband's health at risk. At any age.

You Want A Husband, Not A Patient

Of course, you pledged the *in sickness and in health* bit. And I know you will live up to that vow if, the universe forbid, the time ever comes. But a hospital gown is not a great look on anyone, especially someone you love. For his sake and yours (men are notoriously bad patients and life is hard enough as it is), you want to keep him as healthy as possible.

24

Yes, I know he does a lot of eating when you're not looking. He is not your puppet. You can't control everything he eats, all his meals and snacks. And that is okay. This book is not about giving up favorite foods. But, as you read below about the 80/20 plan, you can do a lot to positively influence his and anyone's health by choosing the foods you do cook for him. And if you make them delicious, which is what this book is all about, he won't feel he is getting medicine at mealtime.

How Do You Get Your Husband to Change His Eating Habits?

Well the first answer to this question is a big negative: Do NOT use the guilt card. If he is like most men (and so many women), telling him he SHOULDN'T eat what he likes is a sure way to send him to the refrigerator for that very item.

I have spent many years trying to convince people (and sometimes myself) to give up or even just cut down on favorite but not very healthy foods. I know it can be a losing proposition if you don't use a little psychology. And guilt doesn't work. You don't want to make mealtime a punishment.

He isn't a bad guy because he likes foods that may be doing him more harm than good. In fact, he is probably very typical. Like smoking, many of us started down the wrong dietary path before we knew it might be hazardous to our health. When processed foods came on the market, we jumped for joy. So did many nutrition experts. Until they started doing the math. Too many ailments were becoming linked to too many foods. But by then, habits had become ingrained. And we know how hard it is to change a habit.

The best way to establish new habits and promote healthy eating is to continually serve delicious meals that just, oh, by the way, are packed with health-promoting ingredients. If the food you serve him tastes good, he won't notice the difference, and won't miss what he isn't eating. Help him relish the healthy foods he does eat, in portion sizes that make sense.

Dr. Brian Wansink, director of the food lab at Cornell University, has done groundbreaking work on why we eat the way we do and strategies for changing our habits. You can check out his work here, http://foodpsychology.cornell.edu/about/brian-bio.html for ideas to help your family make course corrections regarding unhealthy eating habits.

A Tip To Promote Portion Size: Small Plates

We know that portion control is essential to maintaining a healthy weight. If your guy has a tendency to load up his plate and not stop eating until it is empty, which is what most of us do, here is a food psychology trick discovered by Dr. Wansink. One of the secrets to eating healthy-size meals is to serve them on small plates.

When we see a large plate with a lot of "white space" around the food, we feel deprived after finishing the meal. Something in our brain says, there wasn't enough food on that plate.

However, Dr. Wansink's work shows that the exact same amount of food—calorie for calorie, morsel for morsel, when served on a smaller plate, where the food is crowded to the edge of the plate, will give us the same sense of satisfaction. This is true even though the amount of food we eat is the same on both plates. Go figure. But it's true.

So put away your man-sized dinner plates, and get out the salad plates. (Actually, old-fashioned dinner plates used to be the size of our current salad plates. See a connection between plate size and the epidemic of growing waist sizes over the years?) And watch your husband get a handle on portion size.

Of course, a better option than trying subterfuge is to get your husband, indeed your whole family, on board with healthy portion sizes. But if that won't work at first, put away your big platters.

The 80-20 Rule Of Healthy Eating

I'm fond of an old saying, *he who walks down the middle of the road, gets hit from both sides.* It means that veering to the left sometimes, and then to right isn't going to hurt anybody. How much veering is wise when it comes to the foods we eat? About 80/20.

There seems to be an 80-20 law in the universe. When businesses look at their profit and loss statements, for instance, they discover that 80% of effort produces 20% of income. Twenty percent of clients or co-workers will cause 80% of the problems. Many aspects of life have an 80/20 relationship.

This observation was discovered by an Italian economist named Pareto around the turn of the 20th century. Over and over it has been demonstrated to be true today.

In fact, in managing a food program, many nutritionists preach 80/20 as well. If you keep 80% of your meals on target, meaning healthy, balanced and full of nutritional, low fat, superfoods, then you can have some leeway with the other 20%.

Now eating 80% "healthy husband" foods does not mean the other 20% can be straight hits of sugar, butter, well-marbled steaks or other foods shown to cause health problems when eaten in excess. Rather, it means you can select 20% of your dishes, whether here or in another recipe collection, that contain any ingredients you like. These dishes will have a blend of items that include non-superfoods, but not have them dominate a meal. A fresh fruit dessert topped with frozen yogurt rather than ice cream; pancakes with fresh fruit sauce rather than a sugary syrup. You get the picture.

How you manage your 80/20 eating plan is up to you. You have roughly 21 meals to play with. Have a rich meal once or twice a week, or eat clean and lean throughout the day but give yourself an indulgence at nighttime. Maybe mashed potatoes with some butter, or some chocolate. Perhaps you would prefer to eat your large meals at breakfast and lunch to power you through the day, and go light in the evening. If your husband is not on a restricted diet mandated by his physician, or on a weight reduction program, this could be the eating plan that works for him, and the rest of the family, by the way.

What This Book Is And What It Is Not

This is not a textbook for people with heart disease. Many of the recipes here fit on a heart patient's diet, but the aim is to provide information to help reduce the development of plaque. It does not promise a cure for heart disease or any other type of disease. Nor is it designed to replace any advice given to you by your health management team.

This is not a diet weight loss book promising magical results. You can certainly find many of those out there. (Whether they can deliver or not is another story.) And The Healthy Husband Cookbook does not assume that you and/or your husband need to lose weight. It only assumes you want to eat healthy meals. However, the information provided can help you maintain and even achieve your weight goals under the guidance of your health care provider.

This is not a book about totally retooling your lifestyle with a program for cutting out smoking, reducing stress and getting in the best physical shape of your life with killer abs. Those goals are best realized with a smoking cessation program, a meditation or other stress-busting course and a membership at your local gym. And if you need those programs, please start them as soon as possible.

The Healthy Husband Cookbook has one goal. To provide you with a collection of recipes that offer maximum healthy nutrition and over the top flavor and satisfaction at mealtime, with foods that can have particular appeal to the male palate.

These recipes are not prescriptions to fix all or any ills. They are to bolster you and your husband's health and help prevent diet-related diseases. If you have health concerns, you must discuss them with your health care providers and follow any recommendations they give about your diet. For instance, you may need to lose a few pounds, or bring your blood pressure down a few notches. And if your health care provider recommends a specific diet for any health issue, you must follow it.

However, if you are in reasonably good health and want to do all you can to make sure your eating habits prevent or minimize lifestyle diseases, these recipes are for you.

The superfoods featured in these recipes can help prevent inflammation that causes plaque to build in the arteries, and certain cancers to form and diseases such as diabetes to get a foothold. Notice the words "help prevent." I do not, nor can any book, promise miracle cures through diet for any medical problem. Your health care providers are responsible for giving you the specific program you need to get and stay healthy. But the foods and recipes recommended in this book should be a part of your husband's and your family's overall health program. Think of these recipes as part of your health partnership to reach the well-being goals you desire. They are leaner and more nutritious than many typical recipes, so you may find yourself naturally burning off extra weight, for example.

So these recipes, along with flu shots, exercise and any other recommendations from your doctor, are your partners in health. This is part of your preventive care. And oh, by the way, it will it taste sooooo good.

A Three-Pronged Eating Plan: Continue to Eat Well, Just Differently

The most important lesson I've learned about diet is that if the food doesn't taste good, no one will eat it no matter how healthy it is.

With the number of delicious foods and recipes available, that is not a problem—at least in The Healthy Husband Cookbook. Delicious-tasting, healthy recipes that men love is the first goal. It is accomplished on three fronts. By:

* Eliminating inflammation-producing foods
* Increasing superfoods
* Reducing unhealthy fats

What Are Inflammation-Producing Foods?

Science has made a valuable discovery in the war on disease. Many ailments, such as heart disease and certain cancers are caused or made worse by inflammation in the body. And a lot of this inflammation is caused by diet. Many websites can elaborate on the specifics of inflammation and the importance of an anti-inflammatory diet. Suffice it to say that inflammation is real and so are the foods that contribute to it.

The foods that cause inflammation are known bad actors. The list may not surprise you. They are processed foods with many chemicals and additives, as well as foods made mostly with white ingredients, such as flour and sugar. And then of course the animal fats, the red meat products that don't do anybody any favors when eaten to excess.

What Are Healthy, Anti-Inflammatory Foods

Foods that fight inflammation are the freshies— fresh fruits and vegetables, as well as certain fish and lean meats and skinless poultry. This food list is the same healthy eating plan that nutritionists have been advocating for decades. And it is the one Mother Nature had in mind when she designed the human body.

But now that we know the price we might have to pay for ignoring an anti-inflammatory diet, we need to pay more attention.

An anti-inflammatory diet can heal or help prevent conditions such as heart disease, certain cancers, and diabetes. The list is long. It is clear that increasing anti-inflammatory foods in a healthy husband's diet is crucial. The recipes in this cookbook will help you both do just that. Next we come to superfoods, a boon in anyone's eating plan.

What Are Superfoods?

When I first heard the term superfoods, it was in an article describing an obscure fungus found in a hard to reach mountain village on the opposite side of the world from where I lived. I don't recall exactly why it was good for me, but I had an image of something scary and nasty-tasting that was not really food as I know and love it. All the article did was turn me off the notion of superfoods. I avoided all mention of them like the plague.

In time, though, it became hard to avoid reading about superfoods. They were showing up in many books and articles all over the internet. So what were they, I wondered, these magic foods? I started my own research. To my surprise, I didn't find many strange-sounding products.

There Is Nothing New About Superfoods

What I discovered was, well, just food. Real food. Wholesome food. The kinds of foods I've been writing about for decades. There is nothing new about superfoods. Oh, yes, there are some exotic-sounding herbs, roots, seeds and funguses that have been shown to be beneficial to humans. But that is because they are plant-based foods. And different plants grow in different parts of the world. So if you find a list of superfoods from South America, it will be different from those found in Kansas.

Superfoods that may seem exotic to a New Yorker or Londoner, such as chia seeds, are common in parts of Mexico. Others, such as kiwi fruit or pineapple, show up on our tables all the time. We may not think of them as superfoods, but they, and many other common foods, really can do wonders for the human body.

Superfoods are the plant foods, like fruits, vegetables, nuts and seeds as well as fish and lean poultry. Think of them as rainbow foods, if you will, with all the glorious colors you see artfully arranged in the produce section of your market. The anti-inflammatory foods are superfoods and vice versa.

Mother Nature Intended Us To Eat Superfoods

Humans have been eating superfoods and anti-inflammatory foods for eons, before the food engineers and manufacturers started adding chemicals to make our foods pest-free, or to give them a long shelf life or make them easy to cook.

The middle aisles of the supermarkets can hypnotize us, luring us with promises of cheap, convenient, processed food products. Why bother with labor and time-intensive fruits and veggies you have to cook from scratch, when you can just throw something packaged in the microwave and have instant dinner?

But now we know better. Superfoods are in the news because they will help us live longer and healthier. Simple as that. The human body was designed to flourish and grow on foods from the plant kingdom because that is where the vitamins and minerals are that we need for survival.

Just as the body was designed to eat healthy food, it was also designed to move. Often, regularly, swiftly. Diet and exercise. The keys to better health. If you don't like the message, blame it on Mom, Mother Nature that is. We can't change our physiology. Not every modern ailment is tied to the foods we eat, but so many of them are that we ignore the connection at our peril.

So What Do Superfoods Look Like, Exactly?

Basically, you will find these recipes full of color. Purple eggplant, blue and red berries, green beans, broccoli and leafy greens, oranges, yams, nuts and seeds. And let us not forget about beans. If you think beans come out of a can bathed in pork and sugar, you are in for a surprise. You will find a new world of legumes opening up. Look for colorful dried beans such as appaloosas and cranberry beans that you can find in many markets and online that are easy to prepare (especially if you have a slow cooker), often conveniently packaged, such as in cans or in the frozen food sections, economical and deliciously filling.

Here is a short list of powerful superfoods common to the western palate. Surprise! Do they look familiar? Of course they do. You may not eat them regularly—I hope this book will change that—but you recognize them from the produce section or spice shelf in your favorite market, right? Some of them you've probably been eating all your life. And the ones that you shy away from? Well I hope the recipes here will tempt you to give them a try.

> Beets
> Cabbage
> Cinnamon
> Turmeric
> Pineapple
> Watercress
> Kale, chard and other greens
> Pumpkin and pumpkin seeds
> Blueberries

Sardines
Anchovies
Prunes

No matter what diet plan you follow or recipes you use, turn to these foods for your meals and snacks as often as you can, hopefully, every day.

So What *Can't* You Feed Your Husband?

You're probably expecting me to land the N-bomb, as in a big, fat NO to foods that taste good or that your husband really, really REALLY likes. Well, I'm not. Unless a health care provider has given him instructions not to eat certain foods in specific quantities, you can feed him anything—as long as you follow the 80-20 rule. Make sure only 20% of the recipes you prepare contain indulgence foods, that is, foods that potentially present problems to the body. Or, use indulgence foods in small quantities. But again, ALWAYS follow the recommendations of medical care providers regarding specific dietary guidelines.

What About Fat

This is not a vegan or vegetarian program. Fish and lean poultry flavor these meals, as well as some beef and lamb. And if you are in the BaCn camp, believing that bacon is so important to the survival of the species that it should be on the Periodic Table, the good news is yes, you can have your bacon and eat it, too. In fact, you can have anything, thanks to the 80-20 rule (see above).

But these recipes do limit animal fat, the cuts of beef, lamb and pork with high ratios of saturated fat. Eating excessive amounts of animal fat and saturated fats, those that remain firm at room temperature, is tied to heart disease and strokes. Studies show that limiting harmful fats reduces your risk (and your husband's) for these nasty ailments. So these recipes use leaner cuts or fattier cuts in smaller portions. Instead of cooking with bacon grease, lard or other unhealthy fats, use monounsaturated oils, such as olive oil, and polyunsaturated oils such as canola and sunflower for cooking and salads.

The 80% Ingredients

You can fill your meals with as much as color as you want—the plant foods, fruits, vegetables, seeds, nuts, roots, whole grains and edible flowers. Fish and lean poultry such as turkey breast can also make frequent appearances on your table. Eggs show up on lists of superfoods because of the low fat protein in the whites and high-density nutrients in the yolks. Use sauces, condiments and flavorings for vegetables that contain limited fats—baked potatoes with yogurt and herbs rather than sour cream, for instance.

The 20% Ingredients

There are more foods you can eat to your heart's content (forgive the pun), than foods you should limit. The 20% ingredients you should limit are easy to remember. They are:

processed foods, such as chips and snacks, or convenience foods such as canned goods with chemicals or ingredients with names you don't recognize or can't pronounce.

white foods, such as processed sugar and flour that have had the nutritional benefit stripped away. Does this mean no sweets or white breads or pastas ever? Not at all, but limit foods made from highly milled and processed ingredients and use more whole grain breads and pastas. Try palm sugar as a sweetener, which is just as sweet and caloric as granulated or brown sugar. Using palm sugar (also referred to as coconut or date sugar) won't help you control calories. But because it has more nutrients than other sweeteners, with a dividend of a deeply satisfying caramel flavor, you do get more nutrition than processed sugar.

unhealthy fats. Healthy Husband recipes call for Canadian bacon, which has almost a third fewer calories than regular bacon. Though regular bacon and pancetta, the Italian cured pork, are essential in a few dishes, you will use them in small quantities that will flavor a dish but not become the main event. Instead of lard, vegetable shortening, butter, margarine and bacon fat, use healthy oils that remain liquid at room temperature. Choose leaner cuts of meat and turn to stews and braises that take advantage of the deep flavor in these cuts. Use marbled cuts in smaller portions and fill out the menu with vegetables, whole grains and salads.

Use Umami, The Flavor Enhancers

As you introduce your husband to new dishes, make sure they are packed with flavor. To help with this goal, think about flavor enhancers, ingredients that pump up the mouth appeal of your food.

Chefs worldwide know that there are certain flavors and ingredients that enhance foods beyond the particular flavor they contribute. They call this principle umami. Some people consider it a separate flavor, like sweet, bitter, salt and sour, though it is hard to find agreement on that score.

What is certain though, is that a pinch of salt, for instance, in a soup, doesn't just add that familiar taste of sodium that we love. It acts like a symphony conductor to bring all the other flavors and ingredients into harmony. Baking soda, which also contains sodium, by the way, would not do that, would it? It does not have the power to meld the onions, herbs, and other savory flavors the way salt does. Salt is umami in action.

There are other umami ingredients that enhance a dish. Parmesan cheese, anchovy and soy come to mind. And so you will be introduced to these flavor enhancers. Not because we want these dishes to taste of fish or soy. But because a pinch, a dash, a squeeze of some of these ingredients will raise your cooking to new heights. And no one will be able to put their finger on exactly what it is that makes a stew or a salad dressing taste so good.

What Superfoods/Anti-Inflammatory Foods Should You Eat Every Day

If you search for a list of superfoods on the internet, you will find a dozen lists claiming to be the definitive superfood list. But when you compare the lists, they don't match. That's because no list is comprehensive, because hundreds of superfoods abound all over the world. No matter where on the globe you live, you will find superfoods. Pick almost anything in the plant world and if it's edible it is most likely good for you.

Some foods that show up on superfood lists are quite expensive, such as maca. They may be hard to find and not suitable for the average family. Sometimes a superfood becomes trendy and it shows up everywhere, such as, currently, chia seeds.

It is not necessary to eat every superfood every day or every superfood in the course of your lifetime. That would not be possible. Eat a wide variety of fresh, local fruits and vegetables, lean meats and fish, nuts, seeds and whole grains, and you will have covered all the bases. Your own research may lead you to items not discussed here. If they appeal to you, give them a try.

Are Some Superfoods Better Than Others

In a balanced diet the answer is no. However, some people follow a diet that rates foods according to a glycemic index. As a result they prize some foods over others, including plant foods. That's fine if you wish to do that, but it is not the focus here. It is important to eat a very wide variety of foods because they each contribute particular, important nutrients. One fruit or vegetable might contain some vitamins and minerals not found in another. So it is necessary to include many healthful items in your diet, even if they are on the wrong end of the index. Besides, you don't want to pass up something that just plain tastes good, regardless of its health quotient.

Compile your own list of favorite superfoods that reflects your family's food preferences and include them in your meals as often as possible.

The Healthy Husband Pantry

I don't expect you to throw out all the foods in your larder, or to prepare everything you eat from scratch. Some cooks do that, those who have the time, money and interest in cooking. Others like convenience foods but might cringe when they buy them, thinking they are not what a "healthy cook" should use.

I'm not in that camp. I love to cook and probably have prepared every complicated recipe from scratch, from boning a turkey to making croissants to devoting the better part of a day to making beef and veal stocks, up to and including straining, restraining and then straining them again to remove every impurity.

I never, however, undertake that kind of cooking when I'm on the run, or when I have a hungry horde demanding a meal. Then I reach for the cans, boxes and frozen food section of my refrigerator. I LOVE convenience foods. Just not the kind that pretends to be dinner or cereal but is nothing but a concoction of chemicals. I am an avid reader of food labels and only buy products with ingredients that my grandmother would recognize as food, as one dietitian described it. No polys, molys or items only described with a number.

When a recipe lists canned tomato sauce, or a frozen vegetable, it is with the understanding that you will read the label and use the healthiest convenience food you can find.

Cooking Tips

I'm assuming you have some familiarity with your kitchen. If that statement surprises you because you believe that every woman knows how to cook a basic meal, I once knew a woman who said she made good reservations and turned her kitchen into a den. I'm not joking. Pity the kids in that family.

However, I want to pass along some tips for healthier cooking and some advice for getting the most out of these recipes. They include a discussion of cooking and salad oils and whether you should use stock or broth.

Choice of Cooking Oil

I have used extra-virgin olive oil as my oil of choice for decades. However, it has a lower smoking point than other oils, so will burn and scorch more easily.

Consequently, I prefer canola oil for cooking. When a choice between olive oil and canola is an option the instructions will call for "canola oil or oil of choice". When olive oil is necessary for the success of a recipe, then it is specified in the list of ingredients. If you prefer the taste of olive oil for cooking, then by all means use it in these recipes. Or, reserve your extra-virgin olive oil for salad dressings, marinades and garnishes, and use canola oil or other oil for cooking. Then, for added flavor, drizzle a spoonful of extra-virgin olive oil over your food or stir it into your sauce before serving.

The Healthy Oils and Why We Love Them

Here is a quick rundown on healthy cooking oils:

Monounsaturated oils, olive and canola, are the heavy hitters on the cooking shelf. They contain the least amount of saturated fat, compared to other fats. They help discourage the body from producing artery-clogging gunk, and can help lower bad cholesterol levels. However, some of the nutritional value of the olive oil is lost when you heat it. That is why it is preferable to cook with canola and drizzle out of the bottle with olive oil. It makes no difference healthwise whether you use plain olive oil, virgin or extra virgin. However, your wallet and taste buds can tell, with some extra virgin olive oils costing as much as a good wine.

Polyunsaturated oils, such as vegetable, corn, soy and peanut oils, are not exactly also rans. They are higher in saturated fat than olive, but still very healthy to cook with and use as dressings, because they still help the body regulate cholesterol levels. We should try to eat a little of these oils every day, at least one tablespoon, because a component, linoleic acid, helps to keep our motors running smoothly. They also have higher smoking points than olive, with sunflower best able to tolerate the heat without breaking down.

A favorite oil of mine is grapeseed oil, mildly flavored and the only oil that helps lower bad cholesterol and raise good cholesterol. Would seem to be a no-brainer to reach for it in the grocery store—if it weren't for the price. I've been trying for years to promote it, hoping increased demand will lower the price, but so far, no luck.

Use your favorite oil of choice in these recipes from the recommended list, unless specifically directed otherwise in a recipe.

Use Chicken Stock or Chicken Broth?

Recipes call for chicken stock and chicken broth, but in these recipes I refer to stock. Is there a difference? There is, and the difference is that stock is homemade and broth is typically commercially made. You can find commercial stock, but not often, and it is more expensive. Stock typically has no preservatives or additives and is made with fresh vegetables, bones (meat, poultry, fish), and various seasonings. It is time consuming but well worth the effort. You achieve a richer flavor without the saltiness of commercial broths. Broths come in liquid and condensed forms, such as cubes and powders, or my personal favorite, the Better Than Boullion.

The days of making stock by hand for all soups and sauces is long gone thanks to commercial food manufacturing. Some of us have never made stock and don't really know the difference. In these recipes I assume you will use commercial broths. The flavor will be more bland than homemade, but only a dedicated chef would know the difference. If you find stocks, use them as first choice, otherwise commercial broths and condensed versions are fine. The one stock I urge you to make because it is so easy is fish stock. You can freeze it and keep adding new stock to it, as you would a sourdough starter.

Okay, that's all the sermonizing. Let's get to the good part, the recipes.

SOUPS

An easy and filling way to include the recommended daily servings of fresh produce, beans and grains is to put them in a delicious, hearty soup. By the way, studies show that people who eat soup before lunch or dinner lose and maintain their weight more easily than people who don't. So simmer a few veggies and beans for health and weight control. The superfoods in this collection include vegetables, garlic, greens and beans. Here are some ideas to inspire you.

Quick Minestrone

The trouble with minestrone is that no matter how delicious it is, the picture never looks as good as the bowlful tastes. Yet, despite its ugly duckling status in my eyes, I will pick a humble but low-fat, healthful minestre over a gorgeous creamed spring pea bisque any day. Well, depends on the creamed pea. When not making it from scratch, use commercial ingredients without harmful additives such as frozen vegetables and canned tomatoes and beans to speed up this nourishing, rich soup. But always use fresh, quick cooking red or fingerling potatoes. This recipe introduces the use of anchovy as a flavor enhancer. You won't taste fish but rather a deep robust flavor permeating the soup. Left over minestrone is even better the next day.

> 2 tablespoons canola oil or oil of choice
> 1 teaspoon anchovy paste, optional, more if desired
> 1 red onion, sliced
> 1 red pepper sliced
> 2 cloves garlic, minced
> 2 large carrots, peeled and diced (or frozen)
> 2 large zucchini, ends trimmed and diced (or frozen)
> 2 fingerling or new red potatoes, diced (unpeeled)
> 1 14-ounce can whole tomatoes, juice included
> 1 15-ounce can white beans, drained but not rinsed
> 5 cups chicken stock
> 1 tablespoon Italian seasoning or Herbes d'Provence

47

4 ounces whole wheat fusilli or other small
  pasta
Salt and pepper to taste
¼ cup grated Parmesan cheese

In a large stockpot, heat the oil until a spray of
water dances on the surface. Add the anchovy
paste, onion, pepper and garlic. Stir for 5 minutes
or until they have begun to soften, but do not
allow to brown.

Add the remaining vegetables, beans and the
chicken stock. Bring to a rolling boil, then reduce
the heat. Stir in the herbs and cook at a lively
simmer until the vegetables are tender, about 30
minutes.

Stir in the pasta, bring to a boil, reduce the heat
and simmer just until the pasta is tender, but not
mushy, about 7 minutes. Season to taste with salt
and pepper.

Serve in bowls with the cheese.

Serves 6

Cream Of Edamame and Lettuce Soup

Edamame has taken the health conscious by storm, and for good reason. Long a favored ingredient in Japanese cooking, the fresh soybean is sweet and packed with protein and nutrients. Often used as a snack garnished with a little salt and Parmesan cheese (some people like the shells as well), edamame makes a bright appearance here in this silky soup, sweetened with lettuce. Some Asian markets carry fresh edamame but look for frozen edamame in your favorite supermarket.

> 2 strips lean, artisan bacon, such as applewood
> 1 teaspoon extra-virgin olive oil
> 1 small leek, diced
> 3 cups edamame (beans not shells)
> 2 cups chicken stock
> 1 cup butter or other sweet lettuce leaves
> 1 cup milk
> Salt and pepper to taste
> Greek-style yogurt or low fat sour cream
> Sprigs of cilantro for garnish if desired

Cook the bacon until cooked until crisp but not browned. Drain on paper towels. When cool enough to handle, crumple and set aside.

In a large saucepan, heat the olive oil until a spray of water dances on the surface. Add the leek and stir over medium heat for 4-5 minutes, until softened but not brown. Add edamame and chicken stock and bring to a boil. Reduce the heat and simmer for 5 to 6 minutes, until just tender.

Add the lettuce and stir just until wilted. Add the milk.

With an immersion (stick) blender, food processor or regular blender, and while still hot, immediately puree until smooth. If desired, thin soup with a little more milk or stock.

Reheat if necessary, stirring constantly. Serve in bowls garnished with bacon, yogurt and cilantro.

Serves 6

Creamy Broccoli and Garlic Soup

Is this broccoli soup or garlic soup? Fifty years ago Julia Child stunned American cooks, used to bland food (IMHO) with 40 cloves of garlic soup. Now we love slow roasted garlic that turns into a mellow, sweet puree. You can peel the individual cloves and simmer them in the stock before adding the potato and broccoli, but it is much easier to roast the garlic and squeeze the mild puree into the soup rather than deal with smelly raw garlic. This is the basic method for a creamy soup, without the cream. For a special occasion, add up to 1 cup of whole milk, half and half or cream and count it as part of your 20% indulgence!

> 1 head of garlic
> 2 tablespoons canola oil or <u>other oil of choice</u>
> 2 leeks, white part only, trimmed, washed and chopped
> 1 roasting potato, such as Idaho, peeled and cut in 2 inch dice
> 1 ½ pounds or large head of broccoli, ends trimmed and cut into pieces (or frozen broccoli)
> 5-6 cups chicken stock
> Salt and pepper to taste
> 4 tablespoons of grated Parmesan cheese, optional

Preheat oven to 400 degrees F.

Slice the head of garlic in half. Rub each half with olive oil (use a pastry brush or rub a little on a paper towel to save your fingers from absorbing the odor), match up the halves and wrap in foil. Place on a baking sheet and roast in the oven for

40-45 minutes or until the garlic is very soft. It must be cooked to a puree or it will still be strong-tasting rather than sweet. You can prepare this several days ahead and store covered in the refrigerator.

Heat the canola oil in a large saucepan until a spray of water dances on the surface. Add the leeks and stir over medium heat until they have softened, about 5-7 minutes. Do not allow them to brown or burn.

Add the potato and chicken stock and bring to a boil. Reduce the heat and cook at a lively simmer uncovered for 15 minutes or until the potato is very tender. Add the broccoli and squeeze in the pureed garlic, discarding the head. Use a small spoon to scoop out the puree if that helps. Raise the heat to a boil, reduce it and simmer for 5-7 minutes until broccoli is still bright green and tender but not mushy.

Puree with an immersion (stick) or regular blender until smooth and creamy. Do not use a food processor or the potato will become gluey. Season to taste with salt and pepper. The soup can be made ahead at this point.

Pour into individual bowls. Sprinkle with the cheese if desired and serve.

Serves 4

Tuscan Bean, Farro and Kale Soup With Chicken

Long prized as a highly nutritious whole grain, farro traces it lineage back to the Romans. Similar to, and often confused with barley and spelt, farro bulks up soups and salads, though you can eat it plain, as you would rice. It is, however, far tastier than rice, at least according to my tastebuds. You can buy farro as a whole grain, either pearled and semi-pearled. The difference is the same as between brown and white rice. The pearled and semi-pearled have the nutritious hull milled away, but they cook faster, 30 minutes vs. 60 minutes. You can cook the whole grain farro and store it in the refrigerator for several days, then just add a cupful to this soup. Use the remainder in salads or stir a flavorful olive oil and some Parmesan cheese into it as a side with grilled fish or poultry. This recipe assumes you will use the faster-cooking farro so make adjustments for either cooked or whole grain.

For a quicker soup, I sometimes use a frozen vegetable mix containing onion, carrots and celery. Kale is a nutrition ninja, one of the most powerful anti-oxidant foods you can eat. However, it releases its heart-health and cancer fighting substances when cooked, so save it for soups and stews rather than salads. Also, kale and calcium don't mix, so take a break in between a serving of kale and dairy products.

> 2 tablespoons canola oil or oil of choice
> 1 large onion, peeled and chopped
> 1 teaspoon anchovy paste, optional
> 3 carrots, chopped
> 2 ribs of celery, chopped

2 garlic cloves, smashed and peeled
4-5 cups chicken stock
1 15-ounce can borlotti or other white
   beans
1 14-ounce can diced tomatoes
1/4 cup chopped flat-leaf parsley
3 sprigs thyme
1 bay leaf
1 cup farro
1 chicken breast, skinless, boneless and
   diced into 2-inch pieces
1 bunch kale, washed and stems trimmed,
   coarsely chopped
Salt and pepper to taste
Freshly grated Asiago or Parmesan
   Reggiano cheese, optional

Heat the oil in a large pot or Dutch oven until a spray of water dances on the surface. Add the onion, anchovy paste, carrots, celery and garlic. Stir over medium heat until they begin to soften, about 10 minutes. Do not let the vegetables scorch.

Add the stock, drained beans, tomatoes, parsley, thyme and bay leaf. Bring to a boil, then reduce to a lively simmer. Add the faro, chicken and kale. Simmer for 30 minutes (see note above regarding cooking time), or until the farro is tender. It will have some bite to it as does al dente pasta. Discard the bay leaf and serve in soup bowls with the grated cheese if desired.

Serves 6

Curried Carrot Soup

While curry powder is the predominant flavor here, I always add turmeric because is a superfood powerhouse. More and more, researchers are discovering the many health benefits of this colorful spice. Though relatively mild on its own, it turns the soup a warm gold and blends well with the flavor of curry.

- 3 tablespoons canola oil or other oil of choice
- 2 leeks, white part only, washed and chopped
- 3 garlic cloves, peeled and smashed
- 3 pounds carrots, ends trimmed, peeled and sliced
- 1 cooking apple such as Gravenstein, cored and chopped
- 6 cups chicken stock
- 1 ½ teaspoons curry powder, or to taste
- 1 teaspoon ground turmeric
- ½ teaspoon dry mustard
- 1 teaspoon ground cumin
- Salt and pepper to taste
- 1 cup half and half or whole milk
- Nonfat plain yogurt or low fat sour cream as garnish

In a large saucepan add the oil and heat until a spray of water dances on the surface. Add the leeks and garlic. Stir until the leeks begin to soften, about 5 minutes. Do not allow them to brown or scorch.

Add the carrots, apple, chicken stock, curry powder, turmeric, mustard and cumin. Bring to a boil, reduce the heat and allow to simmer for 20 minutes or until the carrots and apple are very tender. Season to taste with salt and pepper.

Puree in a blender or with a immersion (stick) blender until smooth. Taste again for seasoning.

Add the half and half or milk and blend until smooth. Reheat and serve hot with a dollop of yogurt or sour cream.

Serves 6

Spicy Chicken Soup with Soba Noodles

Made from buckwheat flour, soba noodles have a nutty taste, more distinctive and flavorful than ordinary white flour pastas. This last minute dish is no more difficult than a quick stir-fry. Make it as hot or mild as you wish by regulating the amount of hot red pepper. Have all the ingredients prepped and at hand before you begin. It comes together quickly and you won't have time to go hunting for the soy sauce half way through. Feel free to substitute vegetables in this versatile soup or use a firm-fleshed fish in place of chicken.

½ pound soba noodles
1 tablespoon peanut oil
4 chicken breasts, boned and skin removed, cut in 1-inch strips
1 tablespoon minced ginger
3 ounces bamboo shoots, cut in thin strips
½ pound shiitake mushrooms, sliced with stems removed
1 red jalapeño pepper, seeds removed and sliced, optional
½ bunch bok choy, chopped
3 green onions, chopped
2 tablespoons light soy sauce
1 tablespoon rice wine or dry sherry
1 teaspoon sugar
1 teaspoon sesame oil
Salt and pepper to taste
8 cups chicken stock
4 tablespoons chopped cilantro

Cook the noodles in rapidly boiling water for 2 minutes or until soft but not mushy. Drain under cold water and set aside.

Heat the peanut oil in a hot wok or skillet until a spray of water dances on the surface. Add the chicken, ginger, bamboo shoots, mushrooms, red pepper and bok choy. Stir constantly over high heat until the chicken is white in the center and the juices run clear, about 2 minutes. Add the onions, soy sauce, rice wine, sugar, sesame oil and a generous pinch of salt and pepper if desired.

Stir in the stock and bring back to a boil. Add the noodles and stir. Taste for seasoning and serve immediately in individual bowls garnished with cilantro.

Serves 4

EGGS

Eggs have been up and down on the nutritional top ten list. Once condemned for the high cholesterol count in the yolk, the humble egg now has pride of place on the superfood/anti-inflammatory table. High in nutrients, low in calories and bursting with flavor, especially if you buy free-range eggs from hens fed undoctored grain, eggs are adaptable to many mealtime preparations, from breakfast omelets to a midnight snack of hard-cooked egg salad.

Here are some delectable eggs dishes to serve at any meal, though because of the high fat content in the yolks, you might have to ration them if you consume other high fat foods during the week. Also remember to count the yolks in baked goods and casseroles.

Chile and Cheese Casserole with Sweet Carrot Salsa

The day that you enjoy this zesty, full-fat cheese dish for dinner is probably not the day to have pork sausage or mac and cheese for lunch. The calorie count for a serving of this casserole is not off the charts, and you can lower it with low fat Cheddar cheese if you wish. This dish is a good example of how to mix higher fat and lower fat cheeses and protein for maximum flavor and moderate fats.

> 1 large baking potato, peeled and thinly sliced
> Salt and pepper to taste
> 5 whole eggs
> 1/3 cup all-purpose flour
> 1 teaspoon baking powder
> ½ teaspoon salt
> 6 large egg whites
> 4 cups plain low-fat cottage cheese
> 2 1/2 cups shredded extra-sharp Cheddar cheese
> 1/2 cup canned chopped mild green chilies
> Sweet Carrot Salsa, recipe follows

Preheat oven to 350°F.

Coat a 9-by-13-inch baking dish with cooking spray.

Place the potatoes in the baking dish and season lightly with salt and pepper. Place in the oven for 5-7 minutes or until they begin to soften and brown slightly.

Meanwhile, beat 2 whole eggs in a large bowl. Thoroughly whisk in the flour, baking powder and salt and then beat in the remaining eggs and egg whites, the cottage cheese, Cheddar cheese and chiles. When the potatoes have begun to soften, remove from the oven and pour the egg mixture over them.

Return the baking dish to the oven and bake until the eggs have set and are custardy in the center, 40 to 50 minutes. Cool slightly before serving with the Carrot Salsa.

Serves 6

Sweet Carrot Salsa

I like to keep this sweet and sour salsa on hand for snacking. I use the mini-carrots here, which you can slice if you like, or use regular carrots, peeled and sliced.

> 1 pound baby carrots
> 1/3 cup water
> 1 tablespoon clover or other honey
> 2 teaspoons butter
> Salt and pepper to taste
> 1/4 teaspoon hot pepper flakes, more or
>   less to taste
> 1 tablespoon lemon juice
> 2 tablespoons each chopped fresh parsley
>   and cilantro

Place all ingredients except the herbs in a covered saucepan and bring to a boil. Reduce the heat and simmer for 5-7 minutes or until the liquid has reduced to a syrup and the carrots are tender but not mushy. Don't overcook or the glaze will scorch.

Remove from the heat and cool slightly. Stir in the parsley and cilantro and serve with the casserole.

Huevos Rancheros with Black Bean Chili and Yams

Enjoy huevos the easy way. Use a high-quality commercial salsa and canned black bean chili such as Goya. Traditionally a breakfast dish, these spiced eggs, beans and yams are so easy and nutritious, they can do double duty on a casual, easy dinner menu as they take almost no cooking. If you prefer, you can scramble the eggs. I like the flavor blend of olive oil and butter here for cooking the eggs. In place of the avocado you can also use guacamole.

Preheat oven to 400 degrees F.

    1 medium size yam
    1 14-ounce can black bean chili, drained if
      it is too liquidy
    4 whole wheat tortillas
    ½ tablespoon extra-virgin olive oil
    ½ tablespoon butter
    4 eggs
    Salt and pepper
    ¼ cup grated queso fresca, Cheddar or feta
      cheese
    1 cup fresh salsa, homemade or
      commercial
    Hot sauce or 1 jalapeño pepper, seeded
      and diced, as desired
    1 avocado diced
    ¼ cup shredded fresh cilantro
    Nonfat plain yogurt or low fat sour cream

Pierce the yam several times with the tip of a sharp knife. Place it on paper towels and microwave on high for 4-5 minutes until soft throughout. Exact time will depend on size of yam. Cool slightly, peel and chop coarsely.

Heat the black bean chili and stir in the yam gently so it doesn't get mushy.

Place the tortillas between paper towels and microwave for 30 seconds or until hot.

In a skillet large enough to hold the eggs, heat the olive oil and butter until melted and add the eggs. Cook for 1 minute or until the white begins to firm up. Season to taste with salt and pepper. Flip the eggs and cook to your desired degree of doneness, runny to firm, up to 2 minutes.

Working quickly, place a cooked egg on each hot tortilla, top with cheese and arrange the chili, salsa, hot sauce and avocado around the egg. Sprinkle with the cilantro. Add a dollop of yogurt and serve immediately.

Serves 4

Sunday Night Vegetable Fritatta

An easy mix of vegetables and eggs that takes little effort after a long weekend of fun and chores. By finely dicing the vegetables, the frittata cooks relatively quickly. I like the vegetables crisp rather than mushy. I love toasting croutons in olive oil or butter to add to a salad or soup. But if I am in a rush, rather than the hard nubs of packaged croutons, I prefer the technique here of cutting up toast and oiling it. You may use either method, depending on your time. A time-saving alternative to chopping the veggies is to use a frozen but partially thawed organic vegetable mix, with some fresh broccoli added. Feel free to substitute your favorite vegetables.

Preheat oven to 400 degrees F.

> 2 slices whole wheat bread
> 3 tablespoons extra-virgin olive oil
> 1 large zucchini, finely diced
> ½ red pepper, seeded and finely diced
> ½ red onion, finely diced
> 3 cloves garlic, minced
> 1 cup broccoli florets, finely diced
> Salt and pepper
> 8 eggs, lightly beaten in a bowl
> ¼ cup coarsely shredded Parmesan
>   cheese, optional

Toast the bread and brush lightly with 1 tablespoon of the olive oil, then cut into 1 inch cubes.

Heat the remaining oil in a large skillet until a spray of water dances on the surface. Add the zucchini, pepper, onion, garlic and broccoli. Stir the vegetables over medium heat until they begin to soften, about 5 minutes. Do not allow them to scorch. While the broccoli is still bright green and the vegetables are soft but not mushy, season to taste with salt and pepper.

Stir the bread cubes into the vegetables and add the eggs. Stir the top of the eggs constantly over medium heat until they begin to settle into the vegetables, about 1 minute or so. You don't want scrambled eggs. With a spatula, lift the bottom of the eggs to allow the uncooked eggs to slide onto the pan but do not overcook.

Place the frittata in the preheated oven for 4-5 minutes or until the eggs are firm. Sprinkle with the cheese, slice and serve immediately.

Serves 4

Pasta with Bacon and Eggs

Better known as Spaghetti Carbonara, this bacon
and egg pasta whips into an easy one-pan meal
loaded with protein and a subtle hint of bacon
deliciousness. Note the dusting of the pasta with
very fine breadcrumbs after draining it. This
allows the sauce to cling to the noodles. If you
only have coarse breadcrumbs, skip this step.
You want powdery-fine breadcrumbs or the sauce
will become "bready." This dish has several
toothsome ingredients—wine, bacon, milk or
cream and cheese. But the amounts are so small
per serving, this still doesn't compare to the
calories and fat in a hamburger.

     1 pound spaghetti
     2 tablespoons canola oil or <u>oil of choice</u>
     1 clove garlic, crushed but left whole
     ¼ cup dry white wine or vermouth, optional
     ¼ pound pancetta or thick applewood or
        other artisan bacon, diced, cooked and
        drained of excess fat
     2 tablespoons very fine breadcrumbs,
        optional
     6 eggs
     2 tablespoons milk or cream
     ¼ cup grated Parmesan cheese
     Salt and pepper to taste
     3 tablespoons minced Italian parsley
     A drizzle of olive oil, optional

Cook the spaghetti in boiling salted water until
tender but not mushy, about 7-8 minutes. Drain
thoroughly and keep warm. If you are making it
ahead, stir in a tablespoon of oil so it will not
congeal.

Heat the oil in a large skillet until a spray of water dances on the surface. Do not allow it to scorch. Add the garlic and wine and boil gently until the garlic softens and is very fragrant. The wine will cook down to about half. Stir the breadcrumbs into the pasta if you are using them and toss until thoroughly coated. Discard the garlic and stir the pancetta and cooked pasta. Into the wine. Heat thoroughly.

Meanwhile, in a small bowl beat the eggs with the milk or cream, the cheese and salt and pepper. Stir the egg mixture into the pasta and continue stirring until the eggs are incorporated into the sauce and well blended. Do not allow them to scramble, but to remain creamy.

Sprinkle with the parsley and serve immediately with extra cheese and a drizzle of extra-virgin olive oil if desired.

Serves 4

Salad Frisee with Salmon and Poached Egg

The French have a word for it, the trick of tucking a poached egg into a meal for added protein. Although that is not the reason they do it, the salad is referred to as frisee. Here we also add healthful salmon. One of the surprises in my culinary life was discovering that you can poach eggs up to a day ahead, cover them with water and plastic wrap and refrigerate. Then just pop them into boiling water for a few seconds to reheat. I've served poached eggs to a crowd using this method and accepted the astonished compliments from guests who imagined I somehow juggled cracking eggs and poaching them while entertaining my guests. Note the instruction to toss the greens with a bit of salt before adding the dressing. This will perk up any salad. This makes a great lunch dish or quick supper.

> 1 tablespoon vinegar, any kind (essential for nicely formed eggs)
> 4 large eggs
> 6 cups of baby lettuces or frisee, washed, dried and torn into pieces
> 1 tablespoon chopped fresh herbs, such as parsley, marjoram, tarragon or chives
> 1 sweet red pepper, finely diced
> 2 slices whole grain toast, brushed lightly with extra-virgin olive oil and cubed
> 2 tablespoons sherry vinegar
> 1 teaspoon balsamic vinegar
> 1 teaspoon Dijon mustard
> A squeeze of fresh lemon
> 1/3 cup extra virgin olive oil
> Salt and pepper to taste

½ pound smoked salmon, coarsely
shredded or good quality canned salmon

Fill a large saucepan with water up to the halfway mark and stir in the vinegar. Bring to a boil and immediately reduce the heat.

Meanwhile, break the eggs one at a time into a cup or small bowl (if a yolk breaks you only have to discard one egg), and slide into a larger bowl. Carefully slide the eggs into the simmering water. Quickly spoon the whites around the yolks to form an oval then leave them alone. Simmer for about 2 minutes. Even if you prefer hard cooked eggs for breakfast, yolks should at least be slightly runny to blend with the dressing.

When the eggs are done, remove them with a slotted spoon and drain on a paper towel. Or, place them in a bowl of warm water if not using immediately. To make them ahead, place in a bowl of water, cover with plastic wrap and refrigerate. To reheat, place in hot water until warm to the touch.

In a large bowl, toss the greens, herbs, pepper and toast cubes with a sprinkling of salt until well mixed.

In a small bowl, whisk together the two vinegars, mustard, lemon juice and olive oil and season to taste with salt and pepper. Add to the salad and toss well with the salmon.

Serve the salad on individual plates and top with a drained poached egg. Season with salt and pepper and serve immediately.

Serves 4

POULTRY

The go-to entrée for so many week night dinners, you can't beat lean turkey, chicken and game hens for ease of cooking and low-fat, high protein goodness. Cut back on fat and calories by discarding as much of the skin as you can before cooking. Also, buy free range poultry to avoid the chemicals and antibiotics mass poultry producers feed their birds. Like sausage, you don't want to know how those birds are bred.

BBQ Chicken Sticklets

I like the wing drumstick at any time. Meaty and flavorful, with this quick, sweet barbecue sauce they almost have me believing I'm eating ribs. So I named them riblets, or should they be sticklets? By any name, they are a lower fat alternative to traditional barbecue, and just as good. Why not regular barbecued chicken? You can use this sauce on a whole, cut up bird. But the wings are perfect as finger food at a party or, if kept on hand in the refrigerator, a protein snack food when dinner is behind schedule.

> 1/2 cup ketchup
> 1/3 cup firmly packed light brown sugar
> 1 tablespoon red wine vinegar
> 2 teaspoons Worcestershire sauce
> 2 teaspoons low salt soy sauce
> 1ablespoon dry mustard
> ¼ cup fresh orange juice
> 2 pounds chicken drumsticks, tips removed
>   and saved for soup

Place all the ingredients except the chicken wings in a covered bowl or jar. Shake thoroughly until mixed.

Place the chicken in a low baking dish larger enough to hold them in one layer. Pour the barbecue sauce over them and turn until they are completely coated. Cover with plastic wrap and refrigerate for at least one hour.

Drain well and place on a hot, well-oiled grill or broiler pan and cook until cooked through and juices run clean.

Serves 6

Five-Spice Grilled Chicken Breasts

An Asian inspired marinade spices up this quick and easy grilled chicken. Serve with black rice and Pineapple Coleslaw to boost your husband's hit of superfoods with both cabbage and pineapple. Don't shy away from using sugar to sweeten marinades. The liquid drains off before grilling and you only get the sweetness, not a slug of sugar. Make sure you brush the marinade on the chicken several times during grilling to keep it moist. This leftover grilled chicken does not age well as the marinade tends to dry out the chicken if left to sit too long after cooking.

Note, always discard marinade that has touched raw meat, fish or chicken before serving to avoid contamination with harmful bacteria. If you use it to brush on the food while cooking, be sure you allow the last application to cook for at least 5 minutes before consuming to kill anything harmful imparted by raw meat or chicken.

  2 cloves minced garlic
  ¼ cup rice wine vinegar
  2 tablespoons soy sauce
  1 teaspoon aromatic sesame oil
  1 teaspoon ground ginger
  ¼ cup brown sugar
  1 tablespoon five-spice powder
  4 boneless, skinless chicken breasts
  4 tablespoons coarsely chopped cilantro

Place all the ingredients except the chicken and cilantro in a small jar and whisk. Place the chicken in a plastic bag and add half the marinade. Shake vigorously until well-blended, massaging the chicken around to be sure it is well coated with the

74

marinade. Rest for at least 10 minutes and up to several hours in the refrigerator.

Drain the chicken and place on a hot, oiled grill. Brush with the reserved marinade and grill the chicken about 8 minutes on each side until it is firm to the touch and the juices run clear. The exact time will depend on the thickness of the chicken breasts. Brush frequently with the marinade for the first few minutes, but be sure the marinade has had time to cook thoroughly before serving. You don't want to serve your diners marinade that is contaminated with raw chicken. Pass the reserved marinade separately.

Serves 4

Penne with Chicken In Tomato Cream Sauce

You can find many versions of chicken stock concentrate to deepen the flavor in this quick sauce, from the old standby bouillon cubes to my favorite, Better Than Bouillon. I spoon a bit of this thick paste into dishes when I want the richness of chicken stock without the liquid. Whatever type you use, read the label and pick one without chemical preservatives.

> 2 ounces whole wheat fusilli
> 2 tablespoons very fine breadcrumbs, optional (See Pasta with Bacon and Eggs)
> 2 tablespoons canola oil or oil of choice
> 1 small onion, coarsely chopped
> 2 cloves of minced garlic
> 1 14-ounce can chopped tomatoes and juice
> 1/4th teaspoon red pepper flakes, or to taste
> Generous pinch of dried oregano or fresh if you have it
> 1/2 teaspoon chicken stock concentrate
> 1 chicken breast, skinless, boneless and diced
> 3 tablespoons heavy cream, optional
> Salt and pepper to taste
> Parmesan cheese, optional

Cook the fusilli in rapidly boiling salted water until it is tender but not mushy. Drain and set aside. Toss with breadcrumbs if you are using them.

Heat the oil in a skillet until a spray of water dances on the surface. Add the onion and garlic and stir over medium heat several minutes until softened. Do not allow the onion to scorch.

Add the tomatoes and juice, red pepper flakes, oregano and chicken concentrate. Bring to a boil and immediately reduce the heat to a simmer. Stir until well blended and cooked through. With an immersion (stick) blender or standard blender, puree until smooth.

Add the chicken and stir frequently over medium heat until cooked through and pale in the center, about 4-5 minutes depending on size of dice. If the sauce is too liquidy, raise the heat to reduce and thicken it a bit. Add the cream and pasta, blend well and season to taste with salt and pepper. Serve immediately with the cheese if desired.

Serves 4

Grilled Sausage with Chopped Salad

To the best of my ability and taste memor, I have recreated the chopped salad served at Market in St. Helena. A favorite Mother's Day lunch spot with my daughter, I always order this salad. Indeed, it is the reason we make the drive from San Francisco, almost two hours! Often I also order the buttermilk fried chicken, but lower fat grilled chicken sausage links are delicious as well. I often find that I have to adjust the seasonings each time depending on the sweetness or bite of the vegetables in the market that week.

> 1 cup raw broccoli florets, finely chopped
> 1 cup raw cauliflower, finely chopped
> 1 carrot, peeled and finely chopped
> 1 stalk celery, finely chopped
> ½ cup red onion, finely chopped
> 2 tablespoons crumbled Bleu cheese
> 2 strips cooked applewood or other artisan
>   bacon crumbled
> 2 tablespoons whole grain mustard
> 1 tablespoon honey or other sweet mustard
> 1 tablespoon extra-virgin olive oil
> 1 tablespoon sherry vinegar
> Salt and pepper to taste
> 1 pound turkey and/or chicken sausage,
>   links as spicy as you like
> 1 tablespoon canola oil or oil of choice

Put the chopped vegetables, cheese and bacon in a bowl and toss thoroughly. Stir in the mustards, olive oil and vinegar. Toss well and season to taste with salt and pepper. May be made ahead and stored covered in the refrigerator for several hours.

78

Heat the olive oil in a large skillet until a spray of water dances on the surface. Add the sausage and stir over medium heat until they begin to brown. Turn frequenly until they are cooked through, about 5-6 minutes. Drain on paper towels.

Serve with the chopped salad on individual plates while the sausage is still hot.

Serves 4

Roasted Grapes and Sausage with Polenta

You don't often see this combination on a restaurant menu outside of Italy, but in my kitchen spicy sausage and sweet grapes are soul mates. You will find versions done the easy way, the sausages quickly sautéed and the grapes added to soften for a few minutes at the end. You can also find this pair done the hard way with a complicated balsamic reduction and wine sauce. This recipe is in the middle. It doesn't require any heavy lifting, but does have some wine and balsamic vinegar to give it some attitude. You can use the packaged pre-cooked polenta chubs (I didn't make it up) that look like fat sausage rolls. Just slice and heat. Or make your own with the recipe that follows.

> 1 tablespoon unsalted butter
> 2 tablespoon grapeseed oil
> 1 pound mixed red and green seedless
>   grapes, washed and stems removed
> 1/2 pound Italian style hot chicken sausage
> 1/2 pound Italian style sweet chicken
>   sausage
> 3 tablespoons balsamic vinegar
> 1 tablespoon fresh oregano
> Polenta, recipe to follow

Preheat the oven to 450 degrees F.

In a skillet large enough to hold the grapes and sausage, add the butter and grapeseed oil. Heat until a spray of water dances on the surface. Add the grapes, and stir for a minute or two.

Place the sausages in the skillet and turn them frequently to allow them to brown for 2 minutes.

80

Add the wine and balsamic vinegar and bring to a boil. Reduce the heat and place in the oven uncovered, turning the sausages and grapes occasionally. Roast for about 10-15 minutes, or until the grapes are soft and have released their juices.

When done, remove the sausages and grapes to a serving platter and keep warm.

Return the skillet to the stove over and stir over medium heat to scrape up the juices for a minute or two and allow the glaze to thicken. Drizzle this syrup over the sausages and grapes, garnish with the oregano and serve hot with polenta.

Serves 4

Perfect No-Stir Polenta

When given a choice between the easy way and the hard way, I'll take easy every time. When it comes to polenta, though, easy means a longer cooking time, during which you can go about your business. It requires no stirring. Seriously. Well, just once. Here's how you do it. The method is simple. You mix polenta, salt and water in an oven-proof skillet. Bake uncovered. Stir just before serving. That's it. You need almost two hours to allow it to bake, but you can make it ahead of time, refrigerate and rewarm before serving. You can use water or stock, but I like fat-free milk for extra richness without fat.. When you take it out of the oven you may stir in butter and/or cheese, or serve plain. You can allow it to cool and become firm, then slice and pan-fry or grill. Anything that you would do with other methods of preparing polenta, you can do with this one.

Preheat oven to 350 degrees F.

4 cups fat-free milk, <u>stock</u> or water
1 teaspoon salt
1 cup polenta

In an oven-proof skillet, combine the water, salt, and polenta and give it one stir just to blend.

Place uncovered in the oven for 1 hour and 20 minutes. You will notice that the mixture will remain watery for most of the cooking period. That's fine. Eventually it will come together. You may notice a skin forming on the skillet. Just ignore that and let it bake away.

After it has cooked for 1 hour and 20 minutes, more or less, stir the polenta and continue to cook for another 10 minutes. Very carefully, the skillet will be VERY hot, remove the polenta from the oven and proceed with the rest of your recipe.

Serves 6

Chicken Roasted with Winter Squash

Even though we think of butternut squash as a winter vegetable, it is available almost all year round. I would serve this on all but the hottest days when you risk getting fined for turning on the oven. If your market offers peeled and diced squash, avail yourself of it to save prep time. Remove and discard as much skin from the chicken as possible to cut down on the fat.

Preheat oven to 400 degrees F.

>   2 tablespoons canola oil or oil of choice
>   3 tablespoons pomegranate molasses, fig vinegar or balsamic vinegar
>   1 large chicken, cut in pieces, as much skin and fat removed as possible
>   1 tablespoon chopped sage
>   Salt and pepper to taste
>   1 medium butternut squash, about 1 1/2-pounds, peeled and diced
>   3 Fuji apples, cored and diced, not peeled
>   1 large, red onion, peeled and cut in eighths
>   2 tablespoons butter
>   ¼ cup white wine, Vermouth, chicken stock or water

Drizzle the olive oil and pomegranate molasses into the bottom of a large roasting pan. Add the chicken, sage and salt and pepper. Toss until the chicken glistens with the oil. Dot with the butter and place in the oven. Roast for about 20 minutes, or until the chicken begins to turn golden. Turn once during this time to coat the chicken with the juices.

Add the squash, apples and onions. Toss thoroughly until everything is coated with the juices. Return to the oven and roast for another 30-35 minutes, or until the squash, apples and onions are tender but not mushy. The chicken should be caramel-colored and the juices run clear when pierced with the tip of a knife or long-tined fork.

With a slotted spoon, transfer the chicken and vegetables to a serving plate and cover with foil to keep warm.

Pour the juices into a fat skimmer and when the fat and juices have separated, discard the fat and pour the juices back into the roasting pan.

Over a medium-high heat on top of the stove, add the wine to the juices in the roasting pan and stir over high heat until they come to a boil. Continue to stir until reduced to about half, and you have a syrupy glaze. Pour any juices from the plate of chicken into the sauce and stir. Spoon over the chicken and serve.

Serves 6

Grilled Turkey Breast Marinated in Wine

Moist and flavorful, this turkey is a nice change from the usual grilled beef and chicken. Sometimes I like turkey without having to cope with the whole bird and the breast is perfect for those occasions. Allow time for the turkey to marinate for at least an hour. Follow marinade precautions described for Five-Spice Chicken.

- 1 boneless, skinless turkey breast, about 1½ pounds
- 3 cloves of garlic, halved
- 1 teaspoon fresh oregano or ½ teaspoon dried
- ½ cup white wine
- ¼ cup extra-virgin olive oil
- 1 tablespoon fresh lemon juice
- 1 teaspoon sugar
- ¼ cup coarsely chopped fresh Italian parsley
- 1 tablespoon each fresh oregano and thyme
- 1 crushed bay leaf
- 3 cloves minced garlic
- ½ cup chopped onion
- Large pinch of cayenne
- Salt and pepper to taste

Rinse and dry the turkey and make 6 slits all over. Insert a piece of garlic and small pinch of oregano into each slit. Place the turkey in a plastic bag.

Add the remaining ingredients and turn the turkey several times it to coat it thoroughly. You may also do this in a bowl with a cover. Place the bag in a bowl to guard against leaks. Refrigerate for 1 hour and up to 24 hours, turning once or twice to coat evenly with the marinade.

Drain and grill the turkey until springy to the touch and the juices run clear when pierced with a knife, about 30 minutes. Exact time will depend on your grill and size of the turkey.

Brush with the reserved marinade after 10 and 20 minutes, but no closer to serving time as per the instructions above. Remove to a platter, slice and serve.

Serves 6

Game Hens with Spiced Fruit and Watercress Salsa

The best way to prepare these simple game hens is roasted in a brick oven. Since not too many home kitchens have one, I also find them quite tasty grilled, broiled or pan-fried. This salsa is a great excuse for the health-giving properties of watercress, an under-used green in my opinion. Use the seasonal bounty, stone fruit such as plums and nectarines in the summer, and crisp pears or apples in the cool months. Just make sure you chop them in a fine dice to release the juices. You also want to add lots of watercress. I find this salsa pleasantly sweet, but if you use tart fruits you can add a spoonful of palm or other sugar. It is rare to find fresh game hens. Look for them in the frozen food section and thaw before cooking.

> 4 game hens, split in half
> 1 tablespoon canola oil or oil of choice
> Salt and pepper
> 2 medium crisp apples, cored and finely chopped but not peeled
> 2 medium kiwi, peeled and chopped
> 1 small orange, peeled and chopped
> 1 cup diced mango or papaya
> 1 cup peeled and chopped jicama
> 1/4 cup diced pineapple
> 1/4 red onion, peeled and diced
> 1/4 teaspoon red pepper flakes, or to taste
> 1 cup shredded watercress

Brush the game hens with the olive oil and sprinkle liberally with salt and pepper. Place under the broiler or on a grill until the juices run clear, about 20-25 minutes, turning frequently.

87

Meanwhile, toss the fruit, onion and pepper flakes in a bowl. Taste for seasoning. Mound the watercress on individual plates and top with the salsa.

When the hens are done, arrange on the plates with the fruit salsa and serve immediately.

Serves 4

MEAT

Healthy diets need to limit animal protein and we are down with that. But we also live in the real world. The average man is not going to give up red meat for all time. So here are five demonstration recipes. They illustrate the ways you can include meat in menus, featuring it in a supporting role, not as the star of the show.

Choose either leaner cuts and use them in stews, or nicely marbled cuts in smaller portions with vegetable and salads to add heft to the meal.

Beef and Bean Burgers with Caramelized Onions, Easy Guacamole and Red Slaw

If beef and beans sound like an odd combination for a burger, think of sloppy Joes, or beef and bean burrito. I like this burger because the beans cut down on fat while adding bulk and fiber. I prefer the sweetness of black beans, but you may like the ease of already mashed refried beans. Either way, this is a winning combination.

> ½ pound ground beef
> ½ cup refried beans or mashed cooked or
>   canned and drained black beans
> 1 small egg
> 1/2 teaspoon ground cumin
> ¼ teaspoon chili powder or to taste
> Salt and pepper to taste
> 3-4 tablespoons corn meal
> 2 tablespoons canola oil
> Whole wheat hamburger buns
> Red Slaw (recipe to follow)
> Guacamole (recipe to follow)
> Caramelized Onions (recipe to follow)
> Mustard, ketchup, pickle or other favorite
>   burger toppings

In a mixing bowl combine the beef, beans, egg, cumin, chili powder, salt and pepper. When thoroughly blended form into four patties and set aside. Broil, grill or pan fry to your desired degree of doneness.

While the patties cook, lightly toast the buns.

90

Place each cooked patty on the bottom half of a bun. Top with the Caramelized Onions, Easy Guacomole and Red Slaw. Cover with the top of the bun and serve immediately.

Caramelized Onions

1 red or Spanish onion, peeled and sliced
Cooking spray

Preheat oven to 375 degrees F.

Place the onions on a baking sheet well oiled with cooking spray. Spread the onion slices in one layer and coat with cooking spray. Turn the onions and spritz the other side. Place in the preheated oven for 15 minutes. Check frequently to be sure they don't scorch. When they start to soften and color, turn the onions and cook for another 5-10 minutes or until golden and caramelized. Remove to a serving dish.

Easy Guacamole

1 ripe avocado, peeled and pit removed
   and discarded
¼ cup commercial salsa, as mild or spicy
   as you desire
3 tablespoons cilantro, coarsely chopped
Juice of half a lime, or to taste
Salt and pepper to taste

In a small mash togethear the avocado, salsa, , cilantro, lime juice, and salt and pepper. Mash together until well blended. Taste for seasoning. Place a piece of plastic wrap directly on the guacomole so it doesn't darken and refigerate until serving time. May be made ahead several hours.

Red Slaw

½ small head red cabbage, shredded
2 carrots, peeled and grated
¼ cup canned beets, diced
¼ cup raisins
1/4 cup olive oil
1 tablespoon sugar
Salt and freshly ground black pepper to
    taste
1 tablespoon fresh orange juice
1 teaspoon finely grated orange zest
1 teaspoon Dijon mustard
1 green onion, chopped

Toss together the cabbage, carrots, beets and raisins in a salad bowl.

In a small bowl whisk together the olive oil sugar, orange zest, Dijon mustard, and orange juice until smooth. Season to taste with salt and pepper. Add the green onion and toss well with the cabbage mixture until well coated. Cover and refrigerate until ready to serve. You can make this several hours ahead.

Thai Sweet and Sour Beef

In creating dishes that would appeal to the robust tastebuds of most men, I needed to replace fatty slabs of beef with something leaner but equally succulent. I chose the leaner top round and deliciously seasoned it with this sweet and sour marinade. I tasted the simple sauce as I experimented with it and frankly, at one point I had my doubts. But this dish comes together at the end with stunning success when all the elements are in place—tart lime, a touch of ginger, a little bite of chili, fresh herbs and a bit of a complex chutney. Couldn't stop eating it. The prep is easy, but beef must marinate at least 4 hours, so this is an ideal make ahead meal.

> 3 tablespoons fresh lime juice, divided
> 3 tablespoons soy sauce
> 3 tablespoons canola oil
> 2 tablespoons brown sugar)
> 1 teaspoon minced garlic
> 1 1/2 teaspoons minced ginger
> 1 1/4 teaspoons red curry paste or chili-garlic sauce, or to taste
> 1 pound top-round London broil or flank steak, about 1 to 1 1/2-inches thick
> 2 red peppers, seeded and sliced
> 6 cups red-leaf lettuce, torn
> 3 shallots, thinly sliced
> 1/2 cup cilantro leaves, chopped
> 1 cup basil leaves, chopped
> 2 cups frozen brown rice, cooked
> 2 tablespoons Major Gray's chutney, large pieces finely chopped

Blend 1 tablespoon of the lime juice (set the rest aside for a moment), the soy sauce, canola oil, sugar, garlic, ginger and red curry paste in a bowl and whisk thoroughly.

Place the meat in a plastic bag or small glass dish and add half the marinade and remaining 2 tablespoons of lime juice (you want the meat tart but the remaining marinade, less so). Cover and refrigerate the remaining marinade to use for the salad.

Seal the bag and massage to coat the meat thoroughly with the marinade. Refrigerate for at least 4 hours or overnight, turning occasionally.

Remove the beef from the bag and allow excess marinade to drain. Place the peppers on a well-oiled grill and cook for 3-5 minutes until softened but not mushy. Add the beef and cook until medium-rare, about 5 minutes per side, or to desired doneness. Set the peppers and beef aside to rest while you prepare the salad.

Blend the rice and chutney and place on a serving platter. Slice the beef thinly across the grain. Place the lettuce, peppers, sliced shallot, cilantro, basil and beef in a mixing bowl, add the beef and toss with the remaining marinade. Arrange over the rice and serve immediately.

Serves 4

Caribbean Pork and Sweet Potato Stew

Small morsels of seasoned pork simmers in a toothsome broth spiced with jalapeño and mellowed with raisins and sweet potatoes. Some of the raisins make way for a sprinkling of gogi berries, those skinny red dried berries jam packed with antioxidants and nutrients. If you cannot locate them in your market, double the raisins. Remember when browning meat, if the oil is not hot enough, the meat will stick to the pan. When started early in the day and allowed to simmer for several hours, this is actually a last minute dish. Also can be made ahead, refrigerated and rewarmed before serving. If you have a slow cooker with an insert that goes from stove to cooker, this is a one pot meal.

> 1/2 cup unbleached all-purpose flour
> 1/2 teaspoon each salt and cinnamon
> 1/4 teaspoon each ground cloves and nutmeg
> Pinch of cayenne to taste
> 1 pound pork tenderloin, cut in one-inch cubes
> 2 tablespoons canola oil or oil of your choice
> 1 yellow onion, peeled and diced
> 2 cloves garlic, minced
> 1 each red and yellow pepper, seeded and chopped
> 1 jalapeño pepper, halved, seeds removed and finely diced, optional
> 1 teaspoon fresh ginger, minced
> 2 cups chicken stock
> 1 cup white wine
> 1 pound carrots, peeled and sliced

2 tablespoons tomato paste
1 bay leaf
1 teaspoon grated orange zest
1 pound sweet potatoes, peeled and diced
1/4 cup raisins
1/4 cup gogi berries
Salt and pepper to taste

Place the flour and seasonings in a plastic bag and shake well to blend. Add the pork and shake until it is completely coated with the flour. Set aside or refrigerate if you are not using it immediately.

Heat half the oil in a large skillet or Dutch oven over medium-high heat until a spray of water dances on the surface. Do not allow it to brown or scorch. Shake off any excess flour from the pork and add to the oil.

Toss and turn the pork in the oil until it has browned, about 5-7 minutes. When it turns golden, remove to a separate dish and add the remaining oil to the pan.

Allow it to warm for a few seconds and then add the onion, garlic, peppers, jalapeño and ginger. Reduce the heat and stir until the onions and peppers begin to soften, about 3-4 minutes. Add the pork, chicken stock, wine, carrots, tomato paste, bay leaf, orange zest and sweet potatoes. Bring to a boil, stirring frequently. Stir in the raisins and gogi berries. Place in the slow cooker on low and cook for 7-8 hours or until the pork is fork tender. Season to taste with salt and pepper. Discard the bay leaf and serve over brown or basmati rice.

Note: if you don't use a slow cooker, simmer the stew for 2-2 1/2 hours or until the pork is fork tender.

Serves 4

Grilled Lamb Chops with Preserved Lemons and Olives

You might want to overlook lamb shoulder for grilling, opting for the fattier, more tender cuts from the leg. But if you did, you'd be passing up the most flavorful part of the lamb, and the leanest. In fact, if you order lamb chops in a restaurant in Greece, where lamb is a national treasure, this is the cut you would get. So don't be afraid to sink your teeth into these chops, as you will have to, for the reward of succulent, flavorful meat. I like these with preserved lemons and olives. You can buy preserved lemons on line, or make them yourself.

> 4 lamb chops cut from the shoulder
> Extra-virgin olive oil
> Salt and pepper to taste
> 1 clove of garlic, halved but not peeled
> ½ cup chopped, pitted olives of choice
> Preserved Lemons, recipe to follow

Rub the lamb chops on both sides with olive oil. Season to taste with salt and pepper and rub the cut side of the garlic over the lamb.

Heat a grill pan with a tablespoon of olive oil until a spray of water dances on the surface. When hot, add the lamb and sear on both sides. Cook until desired degree of doneness, about three minutes on each side.

Just before they are done, add the olives to the pan and heat through. Serve the lamb and olives with the preserved lemons.

Preserved Lemons

About 1 dozen lemons, washed, stems
  removed
½ cup kosher salt
½ cup lemon juice

Thoroughly wash enough lemons to fit tightly in a sterilized quart canning jar. The number of lemons isn't important but you want them really packed in. Scatter about two tablespoons of salt in the bottom of jar. Cut the lemons in quarters but leave them attached at the bottom. Reform them into lemon shapes and pack down tightly in the jar. They should squeeze into one another to extract the juice. Add the reminder of ½ cup of salt. Add the fresh lemon juice up to the top of the jar. Seal the jar and allow to sit on a counter for about 4 weeks.

To use, cut in 1 inch pieces and serve in spoonfuls. They last indefinitely, but when you taste the sweet, tender lemons, they will end up in every meal you serve.

Serves 4

Stir-Fried Beef And Broccoli

I've spent many years trying to recreate the dishes of the old Ming's Restaurant, originally in Atherton on the San Francisco Peninsula, then later in Palo Alto, their second home. Long ago I set out a happy chore for myself, that of attempting to mimic their beef and broccoli. Beef and Broccoli? Ho hum you say. Really? Wait until you taste this one. You need three bowls to assemble the sauce and marinades. Have everything ready before you start to cook because this delicious dish comes together quickly. Note: this dish is salty. If that is a problem for you, marinate the beef in half low sodium soy sauce and half white wine. If you use fresh water chestnuts, peel and slice them and store them in cold water until ready to use.

Step One:
3 tablespoons soy sauce
Light dusting of white pepper
1 1/2 pounds flank steak, cut with the grain in 2-inch-wide strips, then cut each into 1/8-inch strips across the grain

Place the soy sauce and pepper in a plastic bag and add the beef. Turn for a few seconds to coat the beef completely. Set aside for 30 minutes or up to 1 hour.

Step Two:
1 tablespoon rice wine vinegar
2 tablespoons chicken stock
5 tablespoons oyster sauce
2 scant tablespoons light brown sugar
1 teaspoon toasted (dark) sesame oil
1 tablespoon fresh ginger, minced
2 teaspoons cornstarch

Blend all ingredients in a small bowl and set aside.

Step Three:
1/2 pound sliced mushrooms
1/2 cup water chestnuts, sliced, preferably fresh
2 medium cloves garlic, minced
1 tablespoon fresh ginger, minced
4 tablespoons peanut oil or vegetable oil
2 carrots, peeled and sliced thickly on the diagonal
1 pound broccoli, cut into small florets, peel and dice the stems
1/3 cup water

Prepare the mushrooms and water chestnuts and set aside. Combine garlic, ginger, and 1 teaspoon peanut oil. Blend well and set aside.

Heat 2 tablespoons peanut oil in a wok or large skillet over medium-high heat until a spray of water dances on the surface. Drain the excess marinade from the beef over the bowl and add the beef to the hot oil. Stir and turn until the beef is brown and cooked through, about 2-3 minutes, but don't overcook or the meat will toughen. If your pan is small, do this in two batches. Remove to a dish and cover with foil to keep warm.

Add remaining oil to the hot pan and stir in the mushrooms, water chestnuts, carrots and broccoli and cook over high heat for about 30 seconds. Add water, cover, and reduce heat to medium. Cook until broccoli has softened but is still crisp, about 2 minutes only. Do not uncover and recover the pan or the broccoli will darken to an army green color.

Add the garlic and ginger mixture. Stir vigorously until fragrant, about 15-30 seconds. Stir the beef into the skillet. Whisk the cornstarch mixture into the beef and broccoli. Stirring constantly over very high heat, cook until sauce has thickened and evenly coats the beef and broccoli, about 1-2 minutes. Again, don't overcook. Mound on a platter and serve, preferably with rice.

Serves 4

Hoisin Pork and Edamame

What's the big deal about soy beans or what the Japanese call edamame (ed-a-may-me)? How about higher levels of protein, fiber, micronutrients and those health-giving omega 3s, those fatty acids that boost cardiac health, among other things. Mostly we get our soybeans in sauces and other preparations, but the fresh beans are so darn good steamed with a little sea salt and Parmesan cheese sprinkled on them that they have become a taste sensation. Here they enhance a quick, tasty stir-fried pork. If you can't locate edamame, substitute snow peas or green beans sliced in 2 inch pieces.

  1 pound boneless pork shoulder, trimmed of
      fat
  2 tablespoons peanut oil
  1/2 cup carrots, thinly sliced on the diagonal
  1/2 cup zucchini, thinly sliced on the diagonal
  6 green onions, sliced in 1-inch pieces on the
      diagonal
  1 cup edamame, shelled or snow peas, green
      beans, trimmed and sliced
  1/4 cup hoisin sauce
  1 teaspoon dark Asian sesame oil
  1 tablespoon grated ginger
  Juice of one orange

Dice the pork into 1-inch cubes and set aside.

Heat the oil in a wok or skillet until a spray of water dances on the surface. Add the carrots, zucchini and onions and stir over moderately high heat until they just begin soften, about 4 minutes. The size of the pieces will determine the exact time. Add the edamame and toss for 2 minutes. Remove to a separate plate.

Add the pork, hoisin, sesame oil and ginger to the pan and toss over medium high heat until the pork is cooked through, about 6 minutes. Return the vegetables to the skillet with the orange juice and toss just until everything is heated through. Serve immediately.

Serves 4

FISH

How do we love fish? Let me count the ways. Well, mostly one way, in addition to flavor. Omega 3 fatty acids, those low calorie, health-giving compounds found in all fish but mostly the flavorful, oily ones like salmon and tuna.

However, your heart will never meet a fish it doesn't love, so experiment with local fish and new species that come to market. There are hundreds of ways to prepare them. Here are a few.

Spicy Glazed Salmon with Peppers and Pineapple

Use the sugar and spice in jalapeño jelly to perk up this quick stir-fried salmon. A good bottled mango salsa works just as well as homemade, but when fresh mangos are soft and plump in the market I like to make my own. Best served with frozen or homemade oven-baked sweet potato fries.

> 1 tablespoon soy sauce
> 1 teaspoon minced fresh ginger
> 1 teaspoon minced garlic
> 1 pound salmon fillet cut into 1-inch thick slices
> Salt and pepper to taste
> 1 tablespoon canola oil or <u>oil of choice</u>
> 1 red pepper, seeded and sliced
> 1 tablespoon jalapeño jelly
> 1/2 cup crushed fresh pineapple
> 1/3 cup mango salsa, homemade, recipe follows, or commercial
> 2 tablespoons chopped fresh cilantro

Blend the soy sauce, ginger and garlic in a small bowl and set aside.

Season the salmon lightly with salt and pepper.

In a large skillet heat the oil until a spray of water dances on the surface. Add the red pepper slices and stir for 3 minutes until they begin to wilt but are still crisp.

Add the salmon, being sure the pan is hot enough or the fish will stick. Turn to coat evenly with the oil and stir the soy, garlic and ginger mixture into pan. Turn and cook 3 minutes on each side or until firm and pink in the center, stirring frequently. Do not overcook.

Add the jalapeño jelly and pineapple and stir until nicely glazed. Remove to a serving platter. Stir the salsa into the pan and cook on high for 30 seconds or just until heated through and slightly thickened.

Spoon over the salmon, garnish with cilantro and serve.

Mango Salsa

1 mango, peeled, seeded and diced
¼ teaspoon salt
Juice of half a fresh lime
1/4 cup diced red pepper
2 green onions, diced
¼ cup cilantro, diced
1 jalapeño, seeded and diced, as much as
   you can stand

You can either finely dice all the ingredients, or place them in a blender or food processor for a few seconds until they are finely and evenly diced. Be careful that you stop before you puree them. Taste for seasoning and allow to rest for at least 15 minutes, preferably longer, for the flavors to meld. This will keep covered in the refrigerator over night. You can add diced fresh pineapple, jicama or apple. This is great as a dip with raw vegetables or tortilla or pita chips or on chicken.

Makes approximately ¾ cup depending on size of mango.

Whole Salt-Roasted Fish

Does this recipe sound scary to you? Well, if you have ever whipped an egg white you can master this superior method of preparing food. Commonly used with fish, salt-roasting is an ancient technique that seals in moisture and flavor like no other method. I first had it at Daniel Bouloud's restaurant in New York where he served a whole branzino, a large flat mild fish. I couldn't wait to try it at home. Now I use it for fish, prawns, beef and poultry. Give it a chance and you will discover a new realm of cooking. I like serving it to men because they regard it as adventurous eating, you know, manly.

The method is quite simple. Have your fishmonger or fisherman clean and scale a fish of your choice. It can be large, such as a three pound bass, or small, a tray of scallops or peeled prawns or a few trout. Mix salt and egg whites (the first time I made this I used water as a binder but prefer egg whites, preferably beaten though that is not necessary if you don't have an electric mixer). It will resemble a meringue. Place half of this mixture on a baking dish, set the fish on top, cover with remaining salt paste. Make sure the edges are sealed and pop in the oven for as long as you would normally roast your item. The crust will turn golden. Bring it to the table whole, crack the crust with as much pomp as you can muster and serve with the freshest, crispest salad possible and new potatoes, preferably clay-roasted.

Preheat oven to 450 degrees F.

> 1 whole 3-pound fish, such as snapper, cleaned and scaled but with skin

1 bunch fresh herbs such as thyme or
  marjoram
4 -5 egg whites
3 cups kosher salt
Extra virgin olive oil for drizzling
1 lemon, cut into wedges

Wash and dry the fish and place the herbs inside, or on top if you are using prawns, scallops or fillets. Have a baking sheet ready just large enough to hold the fish.

Beat the egg whites until they hold a soft peak. They should be firmer rather than just foamy but not too stiff.

Sprinkle half the salt over the egg whites and with a large spatula or mixing spoon, just turn the whites over onto themselves to fold in salt. Repeat with the rest of the salt. If you don't have a mixer, whisk the egg whites and salt together in a bowl as vigorously as you can.

Spread half of this mortar-like paste on the baking sheet, roughly in the shape of the fish. Set the fish on top and cover with the remaining egg mixture. Make sure you seal the edges.

Place in the oven for 20-25 minutes. Set the baking dish on trivets on your table, ask for a drum roll, crack the crust, discard it and serve.

Serves 6

Grilled Snapper Teriyaki

I like to keep a jar of this teriyaki sauce in the refrigerator to paint on beef, fish, chicken or pork for a quick grill or broil. I've been using it forever and it is hands down the best I've ever had. Serve with brown rice to soak up the juices.

> 2 cloves garlic, crushed
> 1/2 cup light soy sauce
> 1/4 cup regular soy sauce
> 1/4 cup water
> 1/4 cup white wine
> 1 coin fresh ginger
> 2 teaspoons granulated sugar
> 1 pound snapper fillets

In a small bowl, blend the garlic, soy sauce, water, wine, ginger and sugar.

Rinse and dry the fish and place in a flat dish large enough to hold it in one layer, but not much larger. Pour half the teriyaki sauce over the fish. Turn it to coat both sides, and refrigerate for at least 30 minutes.

Drain the fish and place on a hot, oiled grill. Cook for 2-3 minutes, turn and cook on the other side. Exact time will depend on the thickness of the fish. Snapper is done when it is firm to the touch and opaque in the center. Do not overcook. Serve immediately and pass the remaining teriyaki sauce separately.

Serves 4

Salmon with Tomatoes and Leeks

I adapted this recipe from the grand French chef, Fernand Point's book, which I devoured in my days as a young cook. Originally created for sole and cooked mostly in butter and tomatoes, I found that it worked equally well with salmon and less butter. You can use dried herbs if necessary, but fresh is preferable.

> 1 pound salmon fillets
> Salt and pepper to taste
> 3 tablespoons canola oil or oil of choice
> 3 leeks, white part only, stems removed, washed and sliced
> 4 medium large tomatoes, stem and end removed, chopped
> 1 tablespoon fresh basil, minced
> 1 tablespoon fresh marjoram
> 1 teaspoon fresh thyme
> 1/4 cup finely chopped Italian parsley
> 1/4 cup white wine
> 1 tablespoon butter, optional

Cut a round of parchment paper or foil, cut to fit the skillet. Wash and dry the salmon and season both sides lightly with salt and pepper. Set aside.

Heat the oil in a skillet large enough to hold the salmon and vegetables. When a spray of water dances on the surface, add the leeks. Stir over medium heat until they soften, 4-5 minutes.

Add the tomatoes, herbs and wine. Bring to a boil and reduce the heat. Simmer until the liquid reduces by half and the tomatoes have thickened but are still juicy, about 10 minutes. Season to taste with salt and pepper.

Place the salmon in the pan and spoon the vegetables over the fillets, covering them as much as you can. Bring to a boil and IMMEDIATELY lower the heat or the fish will overcook.

Press the parchment paper or foil down around the fish and cover the skillet. (The paper or foil allows the fish to cook on both sides). Simmer for a total of 8-10 minutes, depending on the thickness of the salmon (10 minutes per inch). Do not overcook.

Remove the salmon to a serving plate and if using, stir the butter into the sauce. Pour it over the salmon and serve immediately.

Serves 4

Olive-Crusted Sea Bass

I once received a marriage proposal after serving this heady dish. I don't promise the same results for any other cook, but it is sure to impress all the same. For a quick prep, buy high quality pitted olives and dice them in a mini food processor if you have one. Toast whole wheat bread until crisp, cool it and then grind in a food processor or blender for instant bread crumbs. I do use olive oil in this dish to highlight the olives and rich fish.

Preheat the oven to 425 degrees F.

> 1 tablespoon extra-virgin olive oil
> 3 tablespoons minced shallots
> ½ cup whole wheat bread crumbs
> ¾ cup pitted and finely diced black olives
> Sprig of fresh thyme
> Salt and pepper to taste.
> ¼ cup extra-virgin olive oil
> 4 ling cod fillets or other firm fleshed fish, skin removed
> Pepper to taste (with the olives you don't need salt)

In a small skillet, heat the olive oil and add the shallots. Stir over medium heat for about one minute or until they soften.

Add the bread crumbs, raise the heat slightly and stir until the bread crumbs begin to crisp, but do not let them scorch. This should take only a minute or so.

Stir the olives into the pan and blend thoroughly. Set aside.

Quickly pour the remaining olive oil into a baking dish just large enough to hold the fish in one layer but no larger. Place the fish in the baking dish and turn to coat both sides. Cover with the olive mixture. Sprinkle with the herbs.

Roast for 8-10 minutes or until the fish is firm to the touch and opaque in the center. Exact time will depend on thickness of the fish, approximately 10 minutes per inch. Serve immediately.

Serves 4

Scallops and Prawns with Cilantro Pesto and Green Pea Guacamole

You will serve the colors and flavors of spring, in this light, flavorful mix of pink and green. I created this dish to cut down on the heaviness of traditional basil pesto and avocado, which would overwhelm the delicate scallops and prawns. So easy, so tasty, so healthful. Oh, and so pretty on the plate. You will find many uses for the pesto and guacamole, from chicken and pork to chips and raw vegetables.

> 1 tablespoon canola oil or oil of choice
> ½ pound large raw prawns, peeled, deveined
> ½ pound large sea scallops, side muscles removed, rinsed of all sand
> Salt and pepper to taste
> Juice of half a lemon

In a large skillet, heat the oil until a spray of water dances on the surface. Add the prawns and scallops and turn frequently until the prawns begin to turn pink and the scallops firm up and turn white. Do not overcook.

Season to taste with salt and pepper and squeeze the lemon juice into the pan. Continue cooking for 2-3 minutes on each side. The exact time will depend on the size of the shrimp and prawns. As with any fish, watch carefully and do not overcook. The scallops can be slightly opaque in the center. They will continue to cook in their own heat. Taste the pan juices and adjust the seasoning, adding more lemon or salt and pepper as desired.

Remove to a serving platter and drizzle with the Cilantro Pesto. Spoon the Pea Guacamole on the side and serve immediately.

Serves 4

Cilantro Pesto

1 cup fresh cilantro leaves
3 sprigs fresh basil
½ teaspoon ground cumin
2 garlic cloves
½ cup canola oil
Salt and pepper to taste

Place the cilantro, basil and cumin in a food processor or blender and chop coarsely. Add the garlic and blend briefly. With the machine running, drizzle in the oil until a smooth puree forms. Add salt and pepper to taste.

If not using immediately, preserve the bright color of the pesto by placing a film of plastic wrap on the surface of the pesto, cover with a lid or second sheet of plastic and refrigerate until needed.

Fresh Green Pea Guacamole

1 cup fresh or frozen peas
½ cup chopped red onion
1 garlic clove
1 tablespoon olive oil
1 tablespoon low fat sour cream
1 tablespoon Greek yogurt
Several drops Tabasco to your taste
½ fresh jalapeño pepper, seeded and
 minced, more or less as desired
Salt and pepper to taste
¼ cup avocado

Juice of 1 lime

Steam, boil or microwave the peas for 1 minute. Do not allow them to overcook and do not cover them or they will darken and lose their bright color.

In a food processor or blender, puree the peas with the remaining ingredients except the lime.

Add the lime juice, a bit at a time, tasting as you go. When you have the desired piquancy, and have adjusted the heat and salt to your liking, set aside until the shellfish are ready. If you make it ahead, place a sheet of plastic wrap onto the surface of the guacamole to seal in the puree so it won't discolor. Then cover the bowl with a second sheet or a lid and refrigerate until serving time. In addition to an accompaniment to the shellfish, you can use this as a dip for pita chips or raw vegetables.

VEGETABLES

This is where healthy eating begins, with the bounty of the plant world. Nutritionists suggest we eat between five and nine servings of fruits and vegetables each day, but don't stop there. To counter a typically western diet heavy with animal fats (does your husband's meal plan sound like this?), dietitians also urge us to limit red meat to twice a week in the modest proportions you find in the preceding recipes. The remaining week's dinners make room for fish, poultry and vegetarian meals. The next several chapters offer vegetables—and fruits—in salads, entrees and drinks. Help yourself. Have seconds. Thirds. Don't stop there.

Clay-Roasted Potatoes

As a first generation Irish-American, I come by my love of potatoes honestly. Of course, that would be true if I were German, Peruvian, Dutch, well, almost any nationality. Potatoes are universally loved, and especially by men. They are a staple food when eating with dairy products, such as buttermilk, are relatively low in calories and chock-full of nutrition. The problem with them, as far as your health is concerned, is the way we dress them up--with butter, bacon, sour cream, heavy cream and cheese. It is true that many varieties of potatoes are rather bland on their own. Small, sweet fingerlings, red and other spring potatoes are the exception to the rule, but we still serve those beauties unnecessarily glopped up with fat and calories. If truth be told, most people wouldn't know what a plain, boiled potato tastes like without their favorite toppings.

I was in that camp myself until I discovered a potato roaster. This is an unglazed clay pot with a cover that comes in many sizes. It's sole reason for being is to turn potatoes into creamy, carb heaven without any fat. Simply place a thin layer of sea or kosher salt on the bottom with some fresh rosemary or thyme if you like, stack the washed and dried, whole unpeeled potatoes, any kind, roasting, fingerlings, you name it, cover and place in a 375-400 degree F. oven. The time depends on the size of your potatoes so you will have to experiment, but between 40 minutes to an hour and a quarter. Then serve them with a light dusting of salt and pepper. Nothing else. The salt and clay trap the flavor molecules inside the potato in a creamy infusion (I'm making this up— not sure of the chemistry but it doesn't matter) that will stun you with it's goodness (that part is absolutely true). Whether or not you are watching your fat and calorie intake, you must track down a potato roaster, rinse it out—never use soap. It is unglazed and the soapy taste will forevermore contaminate your food. Just rinse it out after you use it. Let it soak in hot water if the salt sticks to the bottom. Dry it out and store it for next time. Note, the salt you use in the roaster does not leech into the potatoes nor do they taste salty.

> 1 pound new red potatoes
> 1-2 tablespoons sea salt or kosher salt
> 1 sprig of fresh rosemary or thyme, optional

Preheat oven to 400 degrees F.

Wash and dry the potatoes but do not peel or slice.

Sprinkle a thin layer of salt on the bottom of the dry roaster. DO NOT USE OIL OR ANYTHNG OTHER THAN SALT AND HERBS IN THE ROASTER. Amount will be determined by the size of your roaster. Sprinkle with an herb if you are using it.

Stack the potatoes on the bottom of the roaster. Depending on the amount you may have one layer or several. You just need to be able to place the lid on the roaster for a tight seal.

Place in a preheated oven for between 40 minutes to 1 ½ hours depending on size of roaster, size and amount of potatoes.

When done, remove lid, brush excess slat from the potatoes and transfer them to a serving plate. When the roaster has cooled, rinse in hot water but NEVER use soap. If any salt scorches and sticks to the roaster, just soak it and use a spatula to remove anything that sticks.

Serve potatoes with a light sprinkling of salt and pepper.

Serves 4

Sausage, Greens and Mushroom Pizza

This could be listed under poultry, for the chicken sausage, but it fits here as well because it is laden with vegetables, making it a husband-healthy pizza. If you use bulk sausage, break it into pieces and add any other vegetables that suit your fancy, such as peppers or even fingerling potatoes, thinly sliced to cook quickly. The greens I would choose would be spinach or chard, but pick your own favorites.

½ pound mushroom caps, rinsed, dried and quartered
1 pound spicy chicken sausage links, diced,
¼ cup cornmeal
Whole Wheat Pizza Shell or Dough
½ cup prepared pizza sauce
1 teaspoon fennel seeds
¼ cup greens, steamed and squeezed dry of all liquid
10 basil leaves, shredded
Salt and Pepper to taste
¾ cup shredded part skim mozzarella cheese, about 3 ounces
¼ cup Parmesan cheese

Scatter the cornmeal on a round pizza baking dish. Place the shell on the baking sheet or roll out the dough in a 12-inch circle and place on the baking sheet. Brush the dough with the pizza sauce and set aside.

Heat the oil in a skillet over high heat and toss the mushrooms until they begin to wilt. If you use a low heat the mushrooms will release a lot of moisture, so keep the heat high and cook briefly. Remove to a dish.

Add the sausage to the pan and toss over high heat for 2-3 minutes or until the sausage begins to brown.

Scatter the mushrooms, chicken, fennel seeds and basil leaves over the prepared pizza pan. Season with salt and pepper. Scatter the cheese and place in a preheated oven for 15 minutes or until the cheese has melted and the sausage is clearly cooked through. Cut into slices and serve immediately.

Vegetable Carousel

Like ratatouille, the French vegetable stew that requires sautéing each vegetable separately before simmering them all together, time consuming but oh so good, this vegetable mélange is even better the next day.

> 1 tablespoon olive oil
> 2 large onions, peeled and sliced
> 3 cloves garlic, minced
> 1 medium eggplant, peeled and sliced
> 3 large tomatoes, trimmed, chopped, juice reserved
> 1 pound zucchini, sliced
> 3 red and orange peppers, sliced and seeded
> 2 sprig fresh oregano
> Salt and pepper to taste
> 1/4 cup chopped fresh basil

Heat the oil in a Dutch oven or soup pot until a spray of water dances on the surface. Add the onions and garlic and turn until completely coated and stir until slightly softened, about 4-5 minutes.

Add the remaining ingredients and bring to a boil. Immediately reduce the heat and cover. Simmer for 30-35 minutes until the vegetables are tender.

Uncover and raise the heat to a boil. Cook until the liquid has reduced and thickened, 10-12 minutes. Season to taste with salt and pepper, garnish with basil and serve.

Serves 4-6

Braised Mixed Greens with Canadian Bacon

Here I give you my secret for getting gritty vegetables and fruits such as berries squeaky clean. Swish them in a bowl of cold water with a splash of vinegar. Rinse under cold water and dirt rolls right off with no vinegar taste. Do you know the difference between regular and Canadian bacon? About half the calories and fat. Add a meaty flavor to this vegetable braise without doing damage to your 80/20 ratio.

> 3 tablespoons canola oil or <u>oil of your choice</u>
> 2 leeks, white part only, cleaned and diced
> 2 tablespoons pound diced Canadian bacon
> 2 garlic cloves, minced
> 1/2 teaspoon red pepper flakes, more or less as desired
> 2 1/2 pounds, approximately, escarole, Swiss chard and kale, washed, trimmed and coarsely chopped
> 1 14-ounce can diced tomatoes
> 1 tablespoon dried oregano
> Salt and freshly ground pepper
> 1/4 cup *panko* (Japanese bread crumbs)
> 3 tablespoons freshly grated Parmesan cheese

In a large ovenproof pot, heat 2 tablespoons of the oil over medium high heat until steaming. Stir in the leeks, Canadian bacon, garlic and red pepper flakes. Continue to stir until the leeks have softened, but do not let them scorch.

Add the greens a fistful at a time and let them cook down until they have begun to soften, 2-3

125

minutes. Stir constantly. Keep the heat high enough to allow the liquid that will accumulate to begin to evaporate.

Stir in the tomatoes and oregano and raise the heat to a boil. Season to taste with salt and pepper and reduce the heat to low. Continue to simmer, stirring occasionally for about 15 minutes or until the stems of the greens are tender and the juices have reduced. If the greens appear too watery, raise the heat and allow to boil down.

Meanwhile, blend the panko and cheese in a small bowl. When the greens appear done, sprinkle over the greens and coat with a light film of olive oil spray. Place under the broiler for 30-40 seconds or until golden and serve.

Serves 4

Swiss Chard with Raisins and Pinenuts

I like chard most ways but particularly in this simmer served with a robust fish dish, such as the Olive-Crusted Sea Bass. A bunch of chard takes up a lot of real estate in a skillet. If you don't have a large enough pan to accommodate the chard, use two smaller ones, or cook it in batches.

> 1 bunch rainbow or green Swiss chard
> 1 ½ tablespoons butter
> 1 ½ tablespoons canola oil or oil of choice
> 1 tablespoon granulated sugar
> 1/3 cup raisins
> 1/3 cup chopped pinenuts, toasted
> Salt and pepper to taste

Wash the chard thoroughly in vinegar water. Rinse and remove the bottom portion of the stems and discard. Chop the leaves coarsely.

In a large skillet, or two small ones, add the butter and oil and heat until a spray of water dances on the surface. Toss in the Swiss chard and stir over high heat until it begins to wilt. Add the sugar and continue stirring until the stems have begun to soften, about 2 minutes.

Stir in the raisins and pinenuts and heat thoroughly. Season to taste with salt and pepper and serve immediately.

Serves 4

Steamed Vegetables with Garlic and Cheese

So often only one vegetable appears on the dinner plate (at home or in a restaurant). It may be carrot night or broccoli night or Brussels sprouts night. Poor you if you don't happen to love the veggie served on a particular evening. A better method is to mix and match. Pick several vegetables whose flavors and textures complement each other. Broccoli by itself is an also-ran for me. But pair it with carrots and summer squash and I can't wait for the next bite. The sharpness of broccoli is tempered by the sweetness of carrots without having to create a sauce or garnish to doll it up. I'll take peas any way I can get them, but if you put them in a little stock, a small dab of butter and some sweet lettuce and thyme and simmer until tender I am in vegetable heaven. Here I use a colorful blend of spring vegetables and wake them up with some pungent garlic. Need I say that each part contributes to the whole nutritionally? The vitamins and minerals the zucchini doesn't have, the carrots and broccoli probably will, for a smorgasbord of nutrition. The quantities of each vegetable are an approximation, as is the mix. Add more of your favorites and fewer of the also-rans as pleases you.

> 2 cloves of garlic, crushed but not peeled
> 2 tablespoons extra-virgin olive oil
> 1 head of broccoli, cut into spears
> 4 carrots, peeled and cut into wide, 3-inch long diagonals
> 4 green onions, ends trimmed

4 medium zucchini or yellow summer
squash, ends trimmed and halved
lengthwise
2 red peppers, ends trimmed, quartered
and seeds removed
2 tablespoons finely chopped fresh herbs,
such as thyme, oregano, Italian parsley
and chives
Salt and pepper to taste
2-3 tablespoons freshly grated Asiago
cheese

Place the garlic in a small mixing bowl or measuring cup and add the olive oil. Allow it to infuse as you prep the vegetables.

Make sure the vegetables are cut into same size pieces or they won't cook evenly. Zucchini cooks more quickly so can be in larger pieces, while carrots and broccoli take longer to cook and should be in a smaller dice.

Place the vegetables in a steamer with an inch of boiling water. Reduce the heat to a simmer. Add the vegetables. Cover and steam for approximately 8-10 minutes or until the vegetables are tender but crisp. Don't remove the lid to test them more than once or you will darken the green vegetables.

Turn the vegetables into a serving dish. Discard the garlic and pour the garlic-flavored oil onto them. Toss with the herbs and season to taste with salt and pepper. Add the cheese and toss once more and serve immediately. If you don't serve them right away, they will be delicious at room temperature, or chilled the next day.

Serves 4-6

Mash of Carrots, Rutabagas and Parsnips with Cranberries

This fall-winter mix will sharpen any meal. The carrots sweeten the pungency of the parsnips and the cranberries complement the rutabagas for a warm, rosy, presentation. The emphasis in nutrition so frequently focuses on greens, but these yellow and orange beauties fill our need for anti-oxidants as well our taste for complex carbs. You can cook them in plain water, or even roast them before mashing, but I like to punch up the rich flavor, so I simmer them in chicken or vegetable stock. This way, you don't miss the gobs of butter called for in so many vegetable mashes.

> 1/2 pound carrots, peeled and chopped
> 1/2 pound rutabaga, peeled and chopped
> ½ pound parsnips, peeled and chopped
> 3 cups chicken or vegetable <u>stock</u>
> 2 tablespoons butter
> Pinch of pumpkin pie spice
> Salt and pepper to taste
> 3 tablespoons dried cranberries

Place the vegetables in a Dutch oven or large saucepan. Add the stock and bring to a boil. If the liquid does not cover the vegetables, add a bit of water.

Reduce the heat and simmer vigorously until the vegetables are fork tender. Drain and with an immersion (stick) or regular blender, or food processor, puree until smooth. Stir in the butter pumpkin pie spice and season to taste with salt and pepper. Stir in the dried cranberries and serve.

Serves 4

Roasted Roots

The easiest way to fit in the required servings of vegetables in the cool months is to stick root vegetables in the oven and let them roast and naturally caramelize while you go about your business. This example uses sweet potatoes, garlic, potato, rutabaga and carrots, but you can come up with any combination that suits your taste buds. Turnips and parsnips, beets, eggplant, an onion or two, or even a winter squash, such as acorn. Note: if you don't have a large enough roasting pan, make one out of foil by doubling a sheet the size of a cookie sheet and folding up the sides to hold everything in.

Preheat oven to 400 degrees F.

> 2 pounds root vegetables, peeled and cut in two inch dice (a mix of yam or sweet potato, white potato, carrots, a dozen or so garlic cloves in their skins, a dozen Brussels sprouts and rutabaga, or, choose from the list above)
> 2-3 tablespoons extra-virgin olive oil
> Coarse sea salt and ground pepper to taste (use more liberally than usual)
> Italian or other herb seasoning

In a large roasting pan arrange the vegetables in one layer. Season with salt and pepper, olive oil and herbs if you are using them. Toss to coat them thoroughly with the oil. Roast in the pre-heated oven for 25-30 minutes or until the vegetables are tender. Exact time will depend on the size of the pieces.

Season to taste with salt and pepper and serve hot, or at room temperature.

Serves 4

Marinated Artichokes with Peas and Thyme

You can serve the obligatory green salad with roast chicken or lasagna, but for a change, try this savory mix of peas and artichokes as an herbal dream of a first course. I like to serve this in lettuce leaves, which act as little bowls to hold the delicious marinade. How healthy is an artichoke? It is a good source of vitamin C, folate and potassium. I like this presentation because the artichokes are flavorful without needing gobs of butter or mayonnaise for dipping.

> 4 medium, artichokes plus 1 lemon, or 1 package frozen artichokes
> 2/3 cup chicken stock
> 1 medium shallot, finely diced
> 1/4 cup Champagne or white wine vinegar
> 1 teaspoon fresh lemon juice
> 1/4 teaspoon salt
> 2 cloves garlic, crushed but not peeled
> A mix of herbs such as, 1 tablespoon each fresh thyme, fresh, minced basil and fresh oregano, or 1 teaspoon mixed dried herbs, such as Herbes de Provence
> 1 teaspoon extra-virgin olive oil
> 1 tablespoon butter
> 1 cup baby green peas, fresh or frozen
> 4 large butter or red lettuce leaves

For fresh 'chokes, remove the stems from the artichokes and with a kitchen shears, snip the tip of each leaf to get rid of the thorn. If the artichoke is fresh, I like to peel the stem and just remove the scruffy tip because the stem can be just as tender and sweet as the heart.

Place the artichokes in a large pot. Cover them with lightly salted water to which you add a quartered lemon. Bring to a boil, reduce the heat and simmer uncovered for 30-40 minutes until the stem is very tender (that means the heart will be too). Drain and cool slightly to handle. You can refrigerate for a day or two before continuing if you like.

Quarter the cooked artichokes and remove and discard the choke. Or, if using frozen, steam them as directed on the package.

Place the cooked artichokes in a saucepan with the remaining ingredients except for the peas and lettuce. Bring to a boil, reduce the heat and simmer for two minutes. Stir in the peas and simmer for an additional 2 minutes. Taste for seasoning, aiming for a pleasantly tart, peppery flavor.

Discard the garlic and serve immediately on the lettuce leaves. Or, refrigerate and serve cold in the summertime.

Serves 4

Spinach Lasagna

What's not to like about lasagna? It feeds a crowd, freezes easily, can be assembled in steps if you are pressed for time. In addition, it usually tastes better the next day. With the push on to cram in more servings of fruits and veggies, we sometimes find ourselves scrambling to work off a deficit at the end of the day. This recipe offers both spinach and tomato sauce, often overlooked as a contribution to our required five. I sometimes use lasagna as a catch all, adding mushrooms, chopped fennel, or carrots. Count them all, for they, too, contain fat-free fiber, vitamins, minerals and antioxidants, all the things you ask of the vegetable kingdom.

Note the potential time savers in this recipe, pre-shredded cheese, commercial tomato sauce if you choose, and uncooked noodles. The liquid in the sauces render the noodles tender by the end of the cooking time, so there is no need to boil them first. I use fat-free cheese here to demonstrate how to cut down on the fat typical of lasagna, but you can opt for whole milk cheese if you like.

A word about the noodles. If you are not used to "no boil" lasagna noodles, I recommend them. Thinner and producing a less starchy lasagna, they also save time and are easier to manage when layering with the sauce and cheese. However, you might also try soaking them in hot water for a few seconds. Many people prefer the texture, though I find using them out of the box a fine alternative. Barillo and DeCecco both make no boil noodles.

Preheat oven to 350 degrees F.

Basic Quick Tomato Sauce (recipe follows)
  or 1 24 ounce jar of favorite marinara
  sauce
White Sauce with Spinach (recipe follows)
12 uncooked lasagna noodles (see note
  above)
2 cups nonfat or low-fat cottage cheese or
  1 cup cottage and 1 cup part skim ricotta
12 ounces grated or thinly sliced fat free
  mozzarella cheese
1/2 cup grated Parmesan cheese

Spread about a 1/3 cup tomato sauce over the bottom of a 9 1/2 by 13 inch nonstick baking or other lasagna pan. Cover with a single layer of noodles, 3 lengthwise and 1 trimmed to fit the end horizontally.

Dot with 1/4th of the cottage/ricotta cheese and spread loosely over the noodles. Spread 1/3rd of the Spinach White Sauce over the cheese. Sprinkle with 1/4th of the mozzarella cheese. Cover with 4 more noodles.

For the next 2 layers begin with 1/3rd of remaining tomato sauce, then cottage cheese, then Spinach White Sauce and end with mozzarella.

For top layer, add remaining tomato sauce, cottage cheese, spinach, mozzarella and top with Parmesan cheese.

At this point you can cover and refrigerate for several hours, or bake in the preheated oven for 55 or 60 minutes, or until the noodles are tender and the top is golden. Let stand for 10 minutes before serving.

Serves 6

Basic Quick Tomato Sauce

You can use this recipe for any dish calling for a marinara-style or tomato sauce. Freeze any leftover sauce.

> 1 tablespoon olive oil
> 1 medium onion, chopped
> 2 large cloves garlic, minced
> 1 32-ounce can crushed tomatoes with
>   tomato puree added
> 1/4 cup fresh basil leaves
> 1 teaspoon dried oregano
> 1 teaspoon dried thyme
> Salt and pepper to taste

Gently heat the olive oil in a skillet or large saucepan. When a spray of water dances on the surface, add the onion and garlic and stir over medium heat until the onion begins to soften, about 1 minute.

Add the tomatoes in puree, herbs, salt and pepper. Raise the heat until the tomatoes begin to bubble. Reduce the heat and simmer for 30 minutes. Taste for seasoning, adding salt lightly if necessary, and pepper heavily. Use immediately or store, covered, in the refrigerator until needed.

Spinach in White Sauce

By adding spinach to the white sauce, a common ingredient in lasagna, the liquid in the spinach is absorbed by the sauce and the finished dish does not become watery. My tip for using frozen, chopped spinach is to squeeze it in a potato ricers. It will become almost dry, and not add any water to your dish.

> 1 teaspoon butter
> 1 large shallot, finely diced
> 2 10-ounce packages frozen, chopped spinach, squeezed of all liquid
> 3 tablespoons Wondra flour (prevents lumps)
> 3 tablespoons chicken <u>stock</u>
> 2 cups low fat milk, heated briefly in the microwave (cold milk will cause the sauce to lump)
> Salt and pepper to taste

Add the butter to a skillet and heat until melted but not brown. Add the shallot and stir a minute or so until the shallot has softened. Add the spinach and heat thoroughly.

Stir in the flour and blend, then immediately add the chicken broth and hot milk. Raise the heat and stir continuously until it comes to a boil.

Reduce the heat to medium and stir for 2 minutes or until thickened. Season lightly with salt, more heavily with pepper to taste. Set aside. If you are not going to use it immediately, place a piece of plastic wrap directly onto the surface of the sauce to prevent a skin from forming.

SALADS

Some people think a salad is a mound of greens swimming in a bottled dressing. To my mind though, it is an excuse to put all your favorite foods together, be they meat, vegetables, grains, fish or fruit. Then toss them with a tangy mix of oil and a favorite mustard, fruit juice, nectar or vinegar to finish up. Whether you serve salad as an addition to dinner or a one bowl meal, you can use your creativity as well as your leftovers to infuse your meals with healthy goodness.

Thai Prawn and Watermelon Salad

Prawns and watermelon are often paired in Thai cooking. Perhaps that is because, in addition to a lovely taste combination, watermelon is one of the best foods for dehydration, a boon in hot climates. After a strenuous workout, while battling the flu, as you endure a hot summer, think pink, that sweet, luscious, juicy restorative. Use frozen brown rice and pre-cooked prawns, frozen or from the market, and a package of premixed greens and you have an easy meal in a bowl brimming with flavor, antioxidants and superfoods.

½ tablespoon minced fresh ginger
1 clove garlic, minced
¼ cup seasoned rice vinegar
¼ cup fresh orange juice
½ tablespoon toasted sesame oil
¼ cup extra-virgin olive oil
½ teaspoon soy sauce
4 cups premixed packaged organic baby greens
1 ½ cups cooked, frozen brown rice
3 cups diced seedless watermelon
½ cup dried blueberries
1 pound cooked, chilled prawns, fresh or frozen and thawed
Salt and pepper to taste
1 tablespoon chopped scallions
¼ cup chopped cilantro
¼ cup chopped purple or green basil
¼ cup cashews

In a small bowl, whisk together the ginger, garlic, vinegar, orange juice, oils and soy sauce. Stir 2/3rds of this dressing into the rice and blend thoroughly. Reserve the remaining dressing for the salad. Taste and season with salt and pepper if desired.

Arrange the greens on a serving platter or individual serving plates and mound the rice on top.

Toss the watermelon, blueberries and prawns with the remaining dressing. Season to taste with salt and pepper. Spoon this mixture over the salad. Sprinkle with the scallions, cilantro, basil and cashews. Season to taste and serve immediately.

Serves 4

Spanish Salad with Watercress, Marcona Almonds, Membrillo and Manchego Cheese

You can't talk about superfoods without talking about watercress. Often scorned as merely a dainty filling for tea sandwiches, watercress is a heavy hitter when it comes to fighting disease and bulking up the body with vitamins, minerals and phytochemicals. Crunchy and tart in this salad, add punch with a crisp apple, and sweetness with membrillo, a delectable quince jelly paste found in Spanish cuisine. If you cannot find quince paste in your market (check the gourmet section or online), substitute plump raisins to add sweetness. Add the almonds to the garlic and oil to bring out their nutty flavor. Leave apple peel on for additional fiber. By the way, a good rule of thumb is to have protein with every meal and snack. The almonds (use regular whole almonds if you can't find delectable Marconas) and cheese perform that function here.

> 1 tablespoon extra-virgin olive oil
> 1 medium garlic clove, crushed but left
>   whole, peel on is fine
> ½ cup stale bread cubes
> 1/2 cup Marcona (Spanish) almonds
> 2 tablespoons sherry vinegar
> Salt and pepper to taste
> 1/4 cup extra-virgin olive oil
> 2 bunches watercress, stemmed and
>   washed
> 4 ounces Manchego cheese, shaved into
>   thin slices
> 1 crisp, green apple, such as Gravenstein,
>   unpeeled, cored and diced

143

4 ounces membrillo (quince paste), diced in 1/4 to 1/2 inch pieces

Heat the olive oil in a small skillet and add the garlic. Heat just until it is warm. Add the bread cubes and toss until slightly toasted and fragrant. Remove from the heat. Stir in the almonds and set aside.

In a small bowl whisk the vinegar, salt and pepper until blended. Add the olive oil and whisk continuously until thoroughly blended. May be made ahead and stored, covered in the refrigerator for several days.

Toss the watercress, cheese, apple and membrillo in a serving bowl. Discard the garlic and add the croutons and almonds to the salad. Next add the dressing and toss thoroughly. Season to taste with additional salt and pepper if desired and serve immediately.

Serves 4

Curried Brown Rice and Quinoa Salad

This fiber and nutrient packed salad is a crowd favorite whenever I show up with it at a potluck. It uses quinoa (qeen-wa), which we now know is the ultimate superfood, the mother grain to the ancient Incas. This tiny grain does the vitamin and mineral dance like many plant foots, but it is also a complete protein. I use frozen brown rice when I need to make this salad at the last minute. Except for boiling the quinoa, there is no other cooking. As you can see from the brief direction, you just add the ingredients, one after the other. Couldn't be easier. When you want to make it ahead, the salad keeps well overnight, covered and refrigerated.

3/4 cups quinoa
1½ cups boiling water
1 1/2 cups cooked brown rice
1/2 cup canola or grapeseed oil
1 tablespoon fresh lemon juice
2 teaspoons red wine vinegar
Juice of 1/2 orange
1 teaspoon granulated sugar
1/4 teaspoon ground cinnamon
1/4 teaspoon ground cumin
1 teaspoon ground turmeric
Salt and pepper to taste
1/4 cup green onions, chopped, white and green part
1/2 cup chopped cashews
1/4 cup Major Gray's chutney, large pieces chopped
1/4 cup raisins
1/4 cup gogi berries
1/2 orange, peeled, sectioned and chopped

Rinse the quinoa and stir into the boiling water. Cook for 12-15 minutes or until the quinoa grains "pop" and you see a small white center with a halo around it. Drain well. This can be cooked ahead of time.

Place the rice and quinoa in a bowl and add the remaining ingredients. Toss well. Taste and season with salt and pepper as desired. Serve chilled or at room temperature.

Serves 4-6

Winter Cabbage Salad with Walnuts, Apples and Gorgonzola

Some folks turn up their nose at cruciform vegetables, the Brussels sprouts and cabbages that provide so many nutrients. It's understandable. If they are not cooked properly, they smell to high heaven. But cook them uncovered just until tender, and they will delight you as a foil for rich cheese and nut dressings such as this one.

Preheat the oven to 350 degrees F.

> 3/4 cup coarsely chopped walnuts
> 1 tablespoon walnut oil (or olive oil if walnut is not available)
> 3 tablespoons extra-virgin olive oil
> 1 garlic clove, peeled and minced
> 3 cups coarsely shredded red and green cabbage
> 1 small fennel bulb, thinly sliced
> 1 small red onion, thinly sliced
> 1 small apple, green or red variety such as Fuji, cored and diced
> 3 tablespoons balsamic vinegar
> 2 ounces crumbled Gorgonzola cheese
> Salt and pepper to taste

Shape a piece of foil into a small bowl just large enough to hold the walnuts. Add the walnuts and oil in one layer and toss until nuts glisten with the oil. Place the foil on a baking sheet in the pre-heated oven for 8 minutes or so or until the walnuts are fragrant and toasted. Do not allow them to scorch. Remove from the oven and set aside to cool in the foil.

Heat the olive oil in a skillet large enough to hold the cabbage just until a spray of water dances on the surface. Add the garlic and stir until it becomes fragrant, about 30 seconds. Add the cabbage and toss until begins to wilt. It will cook down but you have to be able to toss it as it cooks. Add the fennel, red onion and apple.

Toss over medium high heat until the cabbage begins to wilt. The apples will soften slightly but still retain a crunch. This will take between 8-10 minutes. Do not let anything scorch. If you don't have a large enough skillet, cook in two batches or two pans side by side.

Stir in the walnuts, balsamic vinegar and cheese. Toss well, seasoning with salt and pepper. Mound on serving individual plates and serve.

Serves 4

Spinach, Bacon And Mushroom Salad

Lower the calories and fat if you wish with Canadian bacon, or if you are ready for a splurge, use an artisan, applewood smoked bacon. Read the labels to be sure it contains no preservatives. Unless you buy packaged, washed spinach, trim the ends and swish it several times in cold water with a splash of distilled or other vinegar added. Rinse thoroughly and watch the grit go down the drain. Remember to dry the spinach thoroughly, true for all salad greens, or the dressing won't adhere.

> 1 clove garlic, peeled and crushed, but left whole
> 3 tablespoons extra-virgin olive oil
> 1 tablespoon red wine vinegar
> 1 tablespoon fresh lemon juice
> 1 tablespoon fresh oregano
> Salt and pepper to taste
> 2 slices applewood or Canadian bacon
> 1 large bunch fresh spinach, ends trimmed, washed and dried thoroughly
> ½ pound mushrooms, sliced
> 1/4 cup croutons
> 1/4 cup Parmesan Reggiano cheese, grated

Place the garlic clove, olive oil, vinegar, lemon juice, oregano and salt and pepper in a small bowl or covered jar. Cover and shake well and set aside to allow the garlic to infuse the oil while you prep the salad.

Place the bacon in skillet and cook over medium high heat for 5-8 minutes until crisp and brown. Drain thoroughly between two paper towels and

149

weighted with a pot. Cut away any extraneous fat and dice.

Place the cleaned and dried spinach in a large salad bowl. Add the mushrooms, croutons, cheese. Season to taste with salt and pepper and serve immediately.

Serves 4

Pineapple Coleslaw

Coleslaw is a beloved picnic and barbecue stable in American cooking. Add fresh pineapple and you will have a superfood bonanza on your plate. Take a little care with the way you prepare the cabbage or you will have dressing soup in the bottom of the bowl. I use the method often recommended for eggplant, which is to salt the cabbage leaves prior to adding the dressing, in this case to remove excess water and avoid a runny dressing that won't cling to the leaves. Unlike many coleslaw recipes, I don't add sugar as the pineapple is sweet enough.

> 1 small head or ½ head large green cabbage
> 2 teaspoons kosher salt
> 1/2 cup mayonnaise, preferably homemade or made without additives
> 2 teaspoons white wine vinegar
> 1/2 cup crushed pineapple, preferably fresh
> 1/2 cup raisins

Shred the cabbage, preferably using a food processor to save time. Place in a large bowl with the salt, toss well and allow to sit for an hour or so. You can leave it for an afternoon.

Rinse the cabbage in cold water, drain and dry on paper towels or in a salad spinner. Place in a salad bowl with the remaining ingredients and toss thoroughly before serving.

Combine all ingredients in a bowl and toss until thoroughly mixed. Chill before serving.

Serves 6

Green Beans, Beets and Orange Salad with Goat Cheese

Beets are such an important superfood that it doesn't seem fair that Mother Nature doesn't make them easer to prepare. My complaint, a weak one actually, is that they turn my kitchen counter/sink and fingers red, whether I peel them before cooking, or handle them after roasting. Roast beets are definitely a vegetable delight, one of my all time favorites. Growing up, I only ate them out of a can. Loved them then and to my surprise, when I became a finicky fresh-is-always-better kind of cook, I discovered that canned beets hold up flavorwise and are so much easier to use in this salad and other dishes. They are so healthy that it is far better to eat the canned version than forgo them altogether because of the trouble of peeling, etc. For fresh beets, wrap them in foil unpeeled, roast at 350 degrees F until tender (time depends on size of beets, 35-45 minutes), cool slightly and slip off the skins. You can also peel them, slice them and boil them similar to cooking carrots, a much faster method. For an extra touch in this salad, if you have the time, toast the almonds on a piece of foil in a 350 degree F. oven for 5-7 minutes or until just golden but not brown. Yum.

> 2 cups cooked, sliced beets
> 2 pounds thin green beans, ends trimmed and left whole
> 4 large blood oranges or honey tangerines, peeled and separated into segments, seeds removed
> Juice of 2 blood oranges or honey tangerines
> 1 teaspoon orange or tangerine zest

3 tablespoons red raspberry vinegar
¼ cup finely diced shallots
1 teaspoon brown sugar
1 teaspoon Dijon or sweet mustard
Salt and pepper to taste
1/3 cup grapeseed or other light oil
4 tablespoons goat cheese

Heat the beets if you are using canned. Steam the beans in a large pot of boiling salted water or microwave them until tender but with a slight crunch. Do not overcook.

Drain the beans into a colander and run under cold water to stop the cooking process and retain the color. Set aside to cool slightly.

Peel and section the four oranges over the bowl to catch the juice for the dressing.

Arrange the oranges and beets on a serving platter with the beans and set aside.

In a small bowl whisk the vinegar, orange juice, zest, shallots, sugar, mustard and oil. Season to taste with salt and pepper. Drizzle over the salad, dot with the goat cheese and serve.

Serves 4

DESSERTS

An end of the meal sweet poses the most perplexing challenge to a cook who wants to cut down on sugar and fat. Fruits offer the easiest option, but sometimes meal planning strategy helps. For instance, instead of an every night low calorie but not very satisfying dessert, offer the old fashioned "kiss the cook" and forgo it altogether. Then pick one night to spend your 20% indulgence and go for the gooey once-a-week extravaganza. Also, you can look at dessert as a way of fitting in an extra daily fruit or two with Ambrosia or any of the other recipes that follow.

Ambrosia

For topping breakfast cereal, for an afternoon snack or for a cool summer dessert, ambrosia treats the palate and heals the body. Cut up your favorite fruits or be adventurous and try an unfamiliar variety when one appears in the market. It's fruit. It can't hurt you. Or, go for the tried and true and fill your bowl with a sample of these seasonal goodies. Try to include at least 4 or 5 varieties.

> 1 cup each blueberries, raspberries and strawberries, washed
> 1 cup strawberries, washed, hulled and halved
> 2 oranges, peeled and sectioned
> 2 spears of fresh pineapple, sliced
> 1 apple, cored and diced
> 1 pear, cored and diced
> 1 mango, peeled and diced
> 1/4 cup apple or pineapple juice
> 1/4 cup shredded fresh coconut, optional
> Vanilla or plain low fat yogurt, optional
> Mint leaves if available

Mix the fruit in a large bowl, and toss with the coconut. Chill thoroughly and serve with yogurt and a sprig of mint if desired.

Serves at least 6 but leftovers will last a day or so covered in the refrigerator. If you plan to leave it longer than that, spoon out the raspberries and strawberries and keep in a separate bowl so that they don't disintegrate.

Serves 4-6

Angel Food Blueberry Lemon Sundae

Okay, I admit it. I am guilty of violating truth in advertising regulations. Sundaes conjure up mountains of fudge sauce and whipped cream and this dessert has neither. However, it borrows from the layering of flavors you find in a sundae so I rest my case. A rose by any other name and all that, the classic matchup of blueberries and lemon comes together here atop toasted, light as air angel food cake. Enough sugar to satisfy your sweet tooth, but not so much to sink your efforts to enjoy healthier desserts.

> 1–1 1/2-inch slice purchased angel food cake
> 1/2 cup fresh or frozen blueberries
> 1-2 tablespoons fresh orange or tangerine juice
> 1 tablespoon sugar
> 1/4 cup lemon gelato or lemon Italian ice, commercial or homemade (recipe follows)
> Sprig of fresh mint for garnish, optional

Toast the angel food cake and place on a serving plate. In a small bowl blend the berries, juice and sugar. Press a few of the berries against the side of the bowl to release their juice.

Place the lemon gelato on the angel food toast. Drizzle the berries over the ice, garnish with a sprig of mint and serve.

Serves 1

Lemon Ice

When I was a child in New York City, nothing cooled the heat of an August summer night like a scoop of the sweet and tart snowy ice served in a paper cup. I have made and tried many versions over the years and I believe Massimo's Limoncello comes closest to recreating my early memories. If you wish to try it on your own, a recipe follows. If you find a recipe for limoncello in a book or online though, beware, as it likely will refer to a delicious lemon liqueur that I find quite dangerous. It tastes so much like the dessert ice that you (read I) can consume a great deal before the alcohol kicks in. Some recipes use limoncello in their sorbet but you have to be careful, because ice with too much alcohol won't freeze. This version is for teatotalers.

The process is quite simple. You make a simple syrup (boiled sugar and water) and add lemon to taste. Cool in a shallow pan, when it starts to freeze you stir it with a spoon, refreeze, stir it with a spoon, refreeze. Just repeat this until you have a snow-like consistency. Yummo!

> Zest (thin, colored, outermost rind) of one lemon
> 3 cups water
> 1 cup sugar
> 1 pinch salt
> 1 cup fresh lemon juice, about 5-6 lemons (use the juice from the lemon you zested.

Combine 2 cups of the water with the sugar in a medium nonreactive saucepan; bring to a simmer over medium heat. Cook, stirring constantly, until the sugar is completely dissolved. Add the salt, stir, and remove the pan from the heat. Stir in the remaining water and let cool to room temperature.

Cover and refrigerate for a minimum of 1 hour. Meanwhile, place a shallow metal 2 1/2 quart container (such as a large cake pan) in the freezer to chill.

Add the lemon juice, lemon peel, and extract to the chilled sugar mixture; stir until well blended. Pour into the chilled metal pan. Place the pan in the freezer for 30-60 minutes, or until ice crystals form around the edges. Stir the ice crystals into the center of the pan and return to the freezer.

Repeat every 30 minutes, or until all the liquid is crystallized but not frozen solid, about 3 hours. Serve, or remain frozen if you don't use it immediately.

Roast Pears with Mascarpone and Cherry Honey

Proof that simple is best, roasting, simply putting pear halves in an oven for half an hour until tender, and then serving with a dollop of creamy mascarpone cheese, the Italian cream cheese, and a drizzle of an elegant honey such as cherry, produces an easy, understated and unforgettable dessert. Pears work in the fall, while stone fruit is just as good in the summer. This is a year-round treat.

350 degrees F.

> 4 Bartlett pears, peeled, halved and cored
> 4 tablespoons mascarpone cheese
> 2 tablespoons cherry honey, or other honey you desire

Place the pears on a baking sheet coated with a light film of cooking spray. Bake for 30-40 minutes until tender when pierced with a knife.

Remove from the oven and cool to room temperature. Place the pears hollow side up on serving plates. Spoon the mascarpone into the center and drizzle with the honey, then serve.

Serves 4

Ricotta Chocolate Mousse

And how happy were you the day they announced that chocolate was a health food? Dancing in the street happy? Here is a delectable way to offset sugar with the healthy antioxidants in dark chocolate and the protein in creamy ricotta.

> 6 ounces dark chocolate
> 1 1/2 cup part skim milk ricotta
> 2 tablespoons sugar
> 2 tablespoons cream
> ½ teaspoon vanilla
> 1 tablespoon Grand Marnier or other
>   orange liqueur, optional
> Fresh strawberries for garnish

Chop the chocolate into coarse, pebble-size pieces.

In a small bowl, mix the ricotta with the chocolate, sugar, cream and vanilla. Taste and add a bit more sugar if desired. Add the liqueur if you are using it, by the teaspoonful, tasting as you go.

Spoon into parfait dishes and chill until ready to serve garnished with the berries.

Serves 4

Berry Shake

I like this shake for the flavor of course, but also for the hit of calcium in all the low and nonfat milk products. Match your yogurt with your berries, or use complementary flavors. Strawberries with banana yogurt, fresh banana with raspberry yogurt.

> 1 cup 1% milk
> 1 cup nonfat vanilla yogurt
> 1/2 cup nonfat berry yogurt
> 1/2 cup fresh or frozen berries, washes and
>   stemmed if necessary
> 1/3 cup nonfat dry milk powder
> 3-4 ice cubes

Place all ingredients in the jar of a blender and puree until creamy smooth. Enjoy.

Serves 1

Strawberries and Cream

I find many uses for this luscious cream. For desserts I add a pinch of sugar and dollop of cream or you can leave them out and serve it on fruit for breakfast. If you don't use much heavy cream in your recipes and don't want to waste a pint just for a tablespoon, put the remainder in an ice cube tray and defrost just as much as you need for a recipe. I freeze cream and milk and, of course, many cheeses, with no ill effects, and even whip defrosted heavy cream.

> 1 pint fresh or frozen strawberries, hulled and halved
> 1 cup low fat cottage cheese
> 1 tablespoon whipping cream
> 1 tablespoon fresh lemon juice
> 4 tablespoons low fat cultured buttermilk
> Sprigs of fresh mint

Place the berries in dessert cups.

Place the remaining ingredients in the bowl of a blender and puree until smooth. Spoon over the berries and garnish with sprigs of mint if desired.

Serves 4

Bon Appetit

Free Gift For You

Don't forget to check out the How To Cook Healthy website at the address below to get my gift to you of 5 free, delicious, sugar free dessert recipes and receive updates, promotions and tidbits you will enjoy.

http://www.helencassidypage.com/ how-to-cook-healthy-in-a-hurry-bonus/

ABOUT ME

My publishing credits include writing two heart-healthy cookbooks with Stanford University cardiologist, John S. Schroeder, M.D. My work has appeared in Gourmet, Bon Appétit, Self Magazine and Men's Fitness, among other magazines. I have written many articles and online columns and have made numerous public cooking demonstrations as well as radio and TV appearances. For many years I ran my own cooking school and did menu consulting for restaurants.

In addition, I write children's books and mysteries under the pen name Cassie Page.

Contact Me

***Go to this link to join our Facebook group: https://www.facebook.com/HowToCook HealthyInAHurry

Follow on Twitter: @hcpbooks

*** If I can answer any questions for you, please contact me at cookhealthyinahurry@gmail.com

Please read my author page for more information about me and my upcoming books and activities.

https://www.amazon.com/author/helenca ssidypage

Medical Disclaimer

The information in this book is for educational purposes only. It is not meant to provide or replace medical advice you may have received. If you are concerned about a medical or health issue, contact your health care provider immediately. If you are pregnant, have a major health issue, are under 18 or over 65, do not embark on any dietary changes without consulting your physician or other health care provider.

The dietary suggestions in this book are not meant to cure an illness. Your first line of defense in promoting good health is always a consultation with your health care provider. Feel free to discuss this book with your doctor or nutritionist and tailor the book and recipes to your own needs.

I know I am repeating myself, but

Please Leave A Review

Reviews are the life blood of ebook writers. You can help me spread the word about The Healthy Husband Cookbook: How To Feed The Man You Love Good Food and Good Health, second in the How to Cook Healthy in a Hurry series. Please give this book a thumbs up. Tell your friends and please give it a positive review on Amazon by going to this website:

http://www.amazon.com/The-Healthy-Husband-Cookbook-Recipes-Health-ebook/dp/B00BEBOW8K

Get all the books in the series:

How To Cook Healthy In A Hurry, Volume 1

eBook version:

http://www.amazon.com/How-Cook-Healthy-Hurry-Recipes-ebook/dp/B00AP980WG/

Paperback version:
www.createspace.com/4318842

My first book in this series offers 50 delicious recipes that require less than 30 minutes in the kitchen and are packed with flavor and nutrition. I even have a testimonial from a 7 year old that his favorite dinner is from this cookbook.

How To Cook Healthy In A Hurry, Volume 2

eBook version:

http://www.amazon.com/How-To-Cook-Healthy-Hurry-ebook/dp/B00C3OHEGE

Paperback version:
www.createspace.com/4517744

By popular demand, more quick and easy recipes.

**How To Cook Healthy In A Hurry,
Volumes 1 and 2**

eBook version:

**http://www.amazon.com/HOW-COOK-
HEALTHY-HURRY-MINUTES-VOLUMES-
ebook/dp/B00DFN0LDA/**

**Paperback version:
www.createspace.com/4337541**

For your convenience, all the recipes in How To
Cook Healthy In A Hurry Volumes 1 and 2 are
compiled into one book.

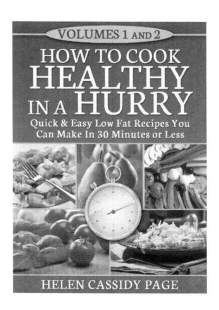

The Soup Diet Cookbook

eBook version:

shttp://www.amazon.com/Soup-Diet-Cookbook-Delicious-ebook/dp/B00BRRZQC2/

Paperback version:
www.createspace.com/4404701

What is the number one problem with losing weight? Hunger pangs. The Soup Diet Cookbook is based on scientific research that shows that certain types of soup eaten at certain times will help ward off hunger. You can lose weight without changing the food you love if you follow The South Diet Cookbook and enjoy the delicious soups and smoothies here.